Information Professionals' Career Confidential

CHANDOS

INFORMATION PROFESSIONAL SERIES

Series Editor: Ruth Rikowski
(email: Rikowskigr@aol.com)

Chandos' new series of books is aimed at the busy information professional. They have been specially commissioned to provide the reader with an authoritative view of current thinking. They are designed to provide easy-to-read and (most importantly) practical coverage of topics that are of interest to librarians and other information professionals. If you would like a full listing of current and forthcoming titles, please visit our website www.chandospublishing.com or email info@chandospublishing.com or telephone +44 (0) 1223 499140.

New authors: we are always pleased to receive ideas for new titles; if you would like to write a book for Chandos, please contact Dr Glyn Jones on email gjones@chandospublishing.com or telephone number +44 (0) 1993 848726.

Bulk orders: some organisations buy a number of copies of our books. If you are interested in doing this, we would be pleased to discuss a discount. Please email info@chandospublishing.com or telephone +44 (0) 1223 499140.

Information Professionals' Career Confidential

Straight Talk and Savvy Tips

ULLA DE STRICKER

AMSTERDAM • BOSTON • CAMBRIDGE • HEIDELBERG
LONDON • NEW YORK • OXFORD • PARIS • SAN DIEGO
SAN FRANCISCO • SINGAPORE • SYDNEY • TOKYO
Chandos Publishing is an imprint of Elsevier

Chandos Publishing is an imprint of Elsevier
50 Hampshire Street, 5th Floor, Cambridge, MA 02139, United States
Langford Lane, Kidlington, OX5 1GB, United Kingdom

British Library Cataloguing in Publication Data
A catalogue record for this book is available from the British Library

Library of Congress Cataloging-in-Publication Data
A catalog record for this book is available from the Library of Congress

Library of Congress Control Number: 2015942341

ISBN 978-0-08-100190-5

For information on all Chandos Publishing
visit our website at http://www.elsevier.com/

Working together
to grow libraries in
developing countries

www.elsevier.com • www.bookaid.org

Cover credit: Cover art by Stephen K. Barringer

Contents

Acknowledgements

As always, I am grateful for all the value I have received from my professional colleagues throughout the years.

Right from the professors in library school on up, I have been the beneficiary of wisdom.

For decades, every colleague I have had the pleasure of working or interacting with has given me fodder for thought.

It has been my privilege to pay it back to colleagues and students by sharing my observations and thoughts. I am grateful for every opportunity.

The comments in this book are meant to stimulate thinking and, I hope, lead to many more conversations.

Introduction

Pull up some chairs. Let's talk about information careers. You may not have realized it at the time you chose the "information profession" ... but with developments in society and technology, your opportunities are getting ever more interesting. For those considering graduate programs in library and information science and for those contemplating a change of profession later on, there are more and new opportunities to pursue.

Many holders of information degrees say when looking back to graduation day that they could not have known what fascinating opportunities lay ahead. Having entered graduate school with a sense that somewhat like law, information science leads to a number of professional roles ... they gladly accepted a job opportunity that came along when they were ready for the job market. With experience, new ones came along. As their expertise grew, they were qualified for an ever wider range of positions.

If you entered an MLS program with the dream of becoming an academic, public, or special librarian, you will find there are of course such jobs to be had. But they are getting fewer in number relative to all the *other* kinds of jobs information professionals are holding now—and you are joined in many cases by hundreds of competing job applicants also pursuing the "pure" path of librarianship as we have known it. By all means keep an eye out for openings in university, public, or corporate libraries ... but indications are you might be wise not to *count on* a steady career there.

- Just take Adele: During graduate school, she discovered her inner nerd in the records management course. Where many people's eyes would glaze over at the mere mention of retention schedules and disposition authorities, she was fascinated. She hadn't seen herself as the "queen of what to keep (for how long) and what to shred," but she found out that records management is a serious corporate challenge and set out to earn her living helping enterprises deal with it. After a series of records manager positions in corporations, Adele became a busy consultant.

- Then there's Carlos: Early on in his career as a museum librarian, he was "voluntold" into a digitization project in which the treasures of the archives were made available to the public. He was smitten. Over time, Carlos became a widely recognized expert in digitizing large collections of historical materials.

- Or take Valentyna: Well into a solid career as a corporate librarian, she took an interest in emerging communication tools and began dabbling in them. Soon, she was an expert being asked to speak at professional events. She, too, set up a consultancy to assist organizations in a large variety of efforts related to communications and marketing.

- Let's not forget Adam: Unafraid of a sales role, he eagerly took a job as a professional publisher's representative. It was his job to explain to customers why they needed the databases and tools on offer, and then to assist customers in the deployment and use of the products and services they had licensed. He became extremely knowledgeable about the ins and outs of content licenses and copyright and moved up to senior roles in large publishing houses and aggregator enterprises, managing intellectual property rights.

There are thousands of such stories. The bottom line for you, the reader: Be confident that your academic information credentials will get your foot in the door ... and that your growing qualifications will move you forward on a professional path you never heard about while you were taking classes and handing in assignments.

My work in the information industry and then my activities as a consultant have given me the opportunity to observe at close range the many roles information professionals are able to fill, and those observations form the backbone of my message to you: *There is a great need in all sectors and industries for your skills ... it's just that you may need to explain to prospective employers how well your expertise fits with the organizational requirements!*

The trick, if you will, is to identify work you find interesting and engaging and to spot opportunities employers may not yet have seen. When you love what you do ... a job doesn't seem like work, and you will naturally give it your all and then some, much to the delight of the employer. There is no point in persevering in a position not providing you professional pride or confronting you with situations you would rather avoid. Right out of school, just about any job is a good one because the bills must be paid. But over time, you will likely gravitate to types of work you find rewarding if—and that "if" is important—you take advantage of any and all opportunities to learn new skills and develop your breadth of knowledge.

My comments in this book are intended to inspire you to find your perfect professional path. I have had the privilege of counseling many colleagues over the years, and I am most grateful to Chandos Publishing for giving me the means of continuing the tradition.

The purpose and use of this book

In previous publications, I have addressed topics related to success in the workplace and in the job market. In this small collection of additional commentary, I share observations stemming from decades of professional work performed at a time when information technology was undergoing rapid and profound change. I have attempted to distill lessons to stand the test of even more change in times to come into a series of suggestions for further thinking as you build your career day by day, project by project, job by job. I trust you will use the myriad resources made available by our colleagues in discussion groups, social networks, and articles and books in order to perfect your marketable skills, and I hope you will see this book as a supplement.

The book is intended as a sampling of considerations in an information professional's career to be discussed in much greater depth in personal conversations. Browse through the book to find the segments most relevant for you at your current career stage; the chapters may be read in any sequence.

My comments are meant to inspire you to pursue or keep developing a career in your chosen subspecialty within the information profession or indeed outside it. I hope to send you on your way with the encouragement that you *will* find the work you always wanted to do—and with a few suggestions for types of work you may not have considered. Aspiring enterprise content managers and newly minted archivists alike have much broader scope of opportunity than they might have perceived during graduate school.

Readers of the Knowledge Management Blog on my website will recognize certain themes I have often raised in postings over the years—the value of being active in professional associations and the ubiquitous presence of examples of knowledge management (or the lack thereof) being just two.

Where relevant in this book, I have incorporated edited excerpts from selected past postings.

At the end of each chapter, I have inserted for the sake of illustration a brief rendition of what would be a conversation typical of many talks I have had over the years with my colleagues. These renditions serve the purpose of briefly shedding light on some specific questions you, too, may have about the points made in the chapter. Though based on my experience, the details in the exchanges are entirely fictional, as are the speakers in them.

Part One
Choosing and Forging an Information Career

What do people think of us? Perceptions of the information profession(s) in society

Knowing how we are perceived in society may turn out to be a significant tool for information professionals forging their careers. Why? Because we may fashion our messages to employers, coworkers in other departments, and the media in ways to counteract the dreaded image of "custodian of old books and keeper of papers in cardboard boxes." We may in many ways emphasize the message that although we manufacture no tangible goods and although we perform services unrelated to or somewhat removed from physical objects or processes, we contribute heavily to the economic life of our community. We are, in fact, members of the "creative class" because we contribute to the development in society and to economic growth—but the onus of explaining that contribution falls on us because we are without a pre-existing reputational framework in society (except, as noted, for an outdated one).

A quick reality check: Say you meet two people at a party and learn they are respectively a veterinarian and a violinist. You would have a strong sense of their professional activities—regardless of the details. In other words, some people can signal with a single word what they do for a living. We can't. The words "librarian" or "information specialist" (regardless of any recognition we may receive as individuals from grateful clients ... as in the advice "be *sure* to befriend a research librarian") do not cover the range of our work; think web content management, enterprise search, data management, records management, competitive intelligence, and everything else we do. Here's another quick reality check: At the party, what responses would you get if you asked "who has been a transformational pioneer in social media?" versus "who has been a transformational leader in librarianship?". It's the nature of the beast—we information professionals tend to work outside the limelight; we do not generally catch mass media attention. You might ask, "does it matter whether we get media coverage for being prominent society influencers?" I say it matters a great deal. Our positive influence could be so much more powerful if it were commonly accepted everywhere in business and public sectors how "our team must include an information professional"—much the way it is often regarded as beneficial to have a lawyer or an accountant on a project team.

1.1 What will library/information/ knowledge graduates be doing 25 years hence? Does it matter right now?

Want to lose track of time for an hour? Here's a suggestion: Just hop online, punch in your personal variation of "librarians obsolete" ... then follow the lively conversations. Naturally, they vary according to the professional specialty being considered—public and corporate librarians, for example, have their own respective aspects of the discussion—tune the search accordingly.

It is quite common to encounter views that every educated individual is a qualified researcher and that corporate memory and enterprise search are a matter for IT professionals using their favorite tools. Lots of great information can indeed be had with very little effort (on the run using mobile devices, no less), and tools for knowledge worker collaboration are indeed eagerly embraced. In such a perceptual environment, it's no surprise former corporate libraries or information centers have had to reinvent themselves so as to offer completely new services (where they weren't simply eliminated, of course). As a result of my professional volunteer activities, I have plenty of occasions to ponder the future of our "tribe." It's inspiring to watch dynamic young professionals succeed ... and yet there are times I wonder whether we are watching a once clearly defined profession (librarians were custodians of knowledge and literature and dished it out or helped others do so) splintering into so many subspecialties it will have trouble remaining and being seen as a definable occupational path. It would be a dream come true to see all my newly graduating colleagues have secure, rewarding, and fulfilling careers ... yet a large dose of realistic assessment will likely be needed: What are the implications of our skills appearing to be subsumed into every other profession? How will evolution in media, communications, and publishing and their underlying infrastructure impact the way in which today's graduates work 25 years hence?

For new graduates and mid-career direction changers, 25 years may be too long a horizon. Finding a suitable job now and keeping an eye on opportunities for the next 3–5 years may be quite enough of a challenge. Better questions, perhaps, are "rather than getting lost in the terminology of my niche specialty, how can I communicate to potential employers what value I bring?" and "how can I avoid being dismissed out of hand because potential employers may have an outdated perception of what my professional skills can do for them?"

1.2 To start, let's take a look at an ultra-brief history of time for information professionals

- In the beginning, we took charge of objects. We stored and protected them and united them with interested consumers. We devised systems for describing the objects and formed networks to track locations of items held elsewhere. We were the keepers of the embodiments of the world's knowledge, and we kept order in the accumulating masses of those objects. We came up with sophisticated systems for enabling the identification of objects relevant to a client's interests and became guides and advisers. For hundreds of years, we figuratively took the hand of our client and laid it upon a printed work saying "this is for you."

- Over time, we came to know that our work is not limited to objects. Rather, we deal in the knowledge *expressed in* objects physical and virtual. We moved into the realm of data and have discussed for decades the attributes of data, information, and knowledge. Simplistically and intuitively, we always understood that data come into being when we notice, record, store, and otherwise deal with observations and measurements (though of course we could ask "does an item of data exist if no one records it?"—just as we ask about the sound of the tree falling unheard in the forest). We took for granted that *information* arises when multiple data items are assembled for a purpose (as we do when we look at temperature values in the context of wind and rain). We instinctively sensed that data and information can be acted upon in an overall framework of *knowledge* made up of information elements (the new

6

homes being built will have specific effects on the so-far observed demand for goods and services in the area). We integrated past experience–knowledge into the judgments or decisions we made (just before the end of the semester, it gets incredibly crowded where the students cram for exams; perhaps we ought to expand opening hours and have extra staff on hand?) and applied it to our work.

- When Knowledge Management came along as a discipline, we created a larger canvas for those concepts and painted onto it our activities to harness all the elements adding up to knowledge. However we labeled those elements, we felt we were uniquely qualified to organize and retrieve them when and where they were needed. We could fetch, assemble, and promulgate recorded knowledge so that others could do with it what they needed or wished to do.

- Since then, we have moved on to collaborating with our clients, partnering in their projects so as to understand their challenges and diagnose tools and solutions to support their objectives. Our understanding of the subject matter at the hand for constituents has given us additional scope for innovation when we apply our specialized expertise as business equals.

- Our future challenge—a view reinforced by many conversations at professional meetings—is to push beyond perceived limitations. We understand data and information and the tools with which to achieve discovery, harvesting, and management. Now, can we step up to influencing positively and constructively the way our clients apply items of knowledge? (You will excuse me for ignoring here the evidence that human beings sometimes act in ways out of line with what experience and learning would suggest. Let the psychologists deal with that contradiction.)

- Knowledge—or wisdom, as some might think of it—is the ability with which we are blessed to *absorb* in order to *apply in action* the insights we take in from others or gather up by observing the world. Knowledge or wisdom is the universe of reference points in which we weigh options, forecast potential outcomes, and otherwise place our confidence in the future. Knowledge influences how we choose to play the game, you could say.

- I see it as our role to enrich and enhance that universe of reference points for others. Not just by filling it with data in warehouses or with information in documents and lists ... but rather by providing a dynamic and responsive environment in which the best inputs, in context we supply, can be applied to decision making by our clients and business partners. Isn't that a very honorable professional role indeed?

1.3 Professional identity in society: What's in a name?

A couple of times within my memory, professional organizations have attempted to devise a name that is at once clearly indicative of the nature of its membership and reasonably pronounceable. The domains in which holders of library and information science degrees are active have broadened in step with the introduction of technologies and tools—so much so that a unifying designation appears to be beyond us.

So who are we? The name discussions reveal that we may each have a strong sense of our own professional identity but that such personal definitions are just that. Much of the sentiment bubbling to the surface touched on "that's not who *I* am," "the proposed new names would be just as incomprehensible to decision makers as the old one was so I'm still at a loss for a clear name," and similar versions of an opinion that we are not solving a problem that has dogged us for as long as we can remember: The fact that our profession is without an image unifying most practitioners. As an example of a profession with such a unifying image, physicians may occupy myriad specialty positions yet are comfortable with the collective name—and they rarely find themselves having to explain to anyone the nature of what they do for a living! But here's the key: Physicians (and members of many other professions) enjoy a pervasive societal understanding of their *role* and the *outcome of their work*. We do not.

We will likely never solve the vocabulary puzzle, for the simple reason that the *impacts we have* are too difficult to characterize succinctly in any way to do them justice. Judging from the many conversations I have had with fellow professionals for decades about our choice of vocation, many of us share the hindsight realization that whatever mental image we may have had when we signed up for graduate school was blown out of the water, if not in our first job then certainly soon thereafter. Never mind, we may have thought: The work is too fascinating and our results too rewarding to worry about what labels we wear.

The discussion confirms observations my colleagues and I have made over many years of project work: It doesn't matter how strategic the work of information professionals is and how expertly it is performed if decision makers' perception is that we are unnecessary. It supports my experience that it is inadvisable to engage in marketing until we have a thorough understanding how we are seen and understood by those who control the budgets: What roles do they believe we fulfill? What difference do they believe our work makes for the organization and its clients and stakeholders? What impact do they think our efforts have on the employees who "do the business of the business?"

As we work to construct our value proposition—associating our expertise and functions with positive outcomes and advantages for the organizations we serve—we can only benefit from paying close attention to the messages and terms that play well in the conversations we have with our stakeholders, just as it is helpful to know what terminology doesn't support our messaging well.

1.4 Influence ... Why don't we have more?

In a time when public libraries are experiencing significant budgetary pressure and corporations and government departments are closing information centers, what influence does our profession have in society?

What influence do we have on public policy and funding for education, social, and health services? Are the librarians—so very familiar with social and educational challenges—consulted when it comes to designing social programs? How can our knowledge be brought to bear on political will?

After all, when new legislation or policy is being drafted, it is customary for representatives of major professions to be consulted: Health care professionals will be consulted in matters related to insurance coverage for drugs; sociologists and law enforcement professionals will be asked for their input if new approaches to young offenders are pondered; teachers and education experts will be called on when school curricula are being revamped or national standards for grade level achievements are on the table.

To be sure, our professions have been represented in discussions about copyright reform, and the kerfuffle arising from certain publisher policies for e-books involved members of our tribe. But overall, many share the view that we *react* (brilliantly, of course) to technological and legislative developments after the fact rather than being called upon to provide input at the earliest possible time.

I do not have ready answers—but in the spirit of "isn't it time we moved from service to influence," I urge reflection: *"How can I, as an information professional, make a positive difference in the legislation and practices of my society?"*

As a profession—in my view—we must expand the definition of what we do. We must adjust our vocabulary to reflect to employers that we are superbly suited in many non-library roles—say, as policy analysts and marketing specialists—due to our skills in data, information, and knowledge management. The desire to work in traditional libraries is, indeed, a respectable goal; it's just that the number of traditional library jobs is dwindling. For many graduates of information schools, the dream of working in a prestigious university library or in a major metropolitan public library may be in need of revision ... into something at least as attractive.

1.5 Is some form of certification the answer?

A quick mental comparison between our profession (whatever we may call it for now) and professions instantly recognized as powerful in society immediately throws up a glaring difference: Physicians are *licensed to practice*, lawyers are *called to the bar*, and engineers *wear that special ring*. In other words, some demonstration of achievement, knowledge, and capacity must be made before members are admitted into the profession and permitted to practice it. Without knowing the details of the exam to be passed, members of the general public understand that those who did pass it are, indeed, distinguished.

Information professionals have no such formal distinction. Once we possess the graduate degree, it remains the only mandatory ticket to many jobs (as in the requirement to hold an ALA accredited MLS, MIS, or MI degree). Granted, there are various specialized certificates to earn (in e.g. records management, privacy, and many more), but they do not carry the pervasive message value held by certified members of the medical, legal, and engineering professions. The bottom line is that the collectivity of the information professions exists without the benefit of the recognition members of regulated professions enjoy.

Similarly, the recognized and certified professions tend to exercise tight ownership and control of professional matters. The medical profession is not about to allow individuals from any other profession to encroach upon what it perceives to be its proper domain; if an individual chooses to see a naturopath or homeopath rather than the family physician, it is a personal choice not necessarily condoned by the latter. In contrast, it has been pointed out how the information profession largely failed to recognize the professional relevance of the Internet when it emerged and allowed all manner of other professionals to "own" it. It has been lamented, for example, that the world would look different today if librarians had taken control and governance of the tool early on. It has been said that librarians excel at adapting new technologies but do not direct their invention and application. All in all, over time the perception of librarianship has become somewhat vague and scattered, sometimes depending on personal exposure to even one librarian: Information specialists not working in public libraries cringe when a famous keynote speaker mentions how "mom took me to the library when I was four years old, and I have loved libraries ever since."

As a result, information professionals of all kinds (from archivists to web masters) lack the kind of clout that puts members of other professions in the hot seat at legislative hearings.

Over the years, the notion of certification has been discussed, but no obvious body has emerged to administer the process. Possibly, one reason is the perceived lack of risk associated with librarianship in action; no concern about injury or death is attached to our work the way such concern is attached to the work of, say, engineers engaged in bridge building or aviation.

Would certification, though, be a means of harnessing the disparate subspecialties into a clear and cohesive community and of providing for members of the public a clearer image of our contribution to society? It is my sense that many information professionals instinctively answer yes. But ... who would undertake the massive amount of work to build and administer the exams (let's leave for now the matter of disciplining or disbarring members violating standards or codes of conduct)? The financial muscle of some professions is absent here, and it is unclear how a certification program would be built and governed. That said, perhaps the challenge will appeal to some among my readers?

1.6 Is it a factor that "anyone can manage information nowadays"?

A related aspect of the vague image we have in society (except for stereotypes) is the common perception that in fact, with the development of technology, we are not needed. Yes, the perception goes, perhaps back in the day when books were rare and precious, it was necessary to have formal keepers; but today, anyone with access to the Internet is a de facto information manager. In many organizations, knowledge workers (those with information centric or intellectual jobs) are expected to find the information they need for their work without the assistance of a professional researcher. Subject matter experts are expected to stay professionally current on their own. Business teams are expected to manage large volumes of documentation (and they certainly do, sometimes with the predictable results of having to rely on shared drives and invented-on-the-fly folder structures).

If the prevailing perception is that our profession has outlived itself, it can be no surprise that we struggle to define ourselves as a valuable group in society. Sometimes, I hear comments that our group lacks universally familiar luminary and inspirational personalities who, through their life-altering achievements, become iconic representatives of a profession (the way Dr. Jonas Salk did through his pioneering polio vaccine work). *We* know who the prominent librarians were and are ... but do the people we meet in our local coffee shop share that awareness?

In that light, we might say it is unfortunate for us that information technology has become everybody's property and that we are rarely associated with heroic accomplishments changing the way people live. (Mind you, it could be daunting to incur the kind of risk associated with managing life or death.)

I raise the matter of our image in society because the absence of the "collective badge" presents challenges as we begin our careers and then develop them later. We are called upon to explain and prove ourselves in quite demanding ways throughout our professional lives. Therefore, we collectively and individually face a lifelong challenge: What will we do, as a profession, to forge a path forward for our members?

1.7 The "Drucker way" future: Opportunity for information professionals to shape it

We owe a great deal of gratitude to Bruce Rosenstein. For some time now, he has dedicated his professional life to extending Peter Drucker's immense legacy through continued (re)interpretation and collaboration with other management experts on the concepts and themes in Drucker's work. In one of his books, he explains the essential difference between an attitude of "the future is unknowable and we can only hope for the best" on the one hand and an attitude of "the future is a mindset and we can have a hand in creating it by understanding it" on the other hand. Bruce calls it being the authors of, not the audience for, the future by maintaining a global world view and staying aware of developments everywhere across the globe (that's what Peter Drucker did); remaining relevant (that's what Peter Drucker still is) and focusing on benefiting others (that was a Peter Drucker principle). They add up to a fundamental message that "current success is not enough … we must organize our future actively."

For information professionals, the direct translation is straightforward—into two questions:

First, if the current [organization, association, work flow, priority allocation, …] did not exist, would we invent it now? In other words, the presence of a certain entity, product, or process today is not necessarily a justification for its future presence. What worked well up to now may not continue to work well. We must be ready, as Bruce says, to "remove and improve." No doubt we have all observed in many contexts how fear of change brings about consequences quite opposite to what the fear of change was supposed to prevent.

Second, are we making sure to expose ourselves to people NOT in our own industry? Bruce Rosenstein describes how Peter Drucker's work—for corporations, unions, nonprofits, and so on—made him "un-pigeonholeable." Seeing so many facets of society and its organizations, Peter Drucker understood all kinds of diverse environments and distilled from them his timeless advice.

When we associate with and expand our knowledge of what professionals in adjacent domains do, new opportunities may become clear as we discover how to bring different skills jointly to bear on societal or organizational challenges. As an example, say an organization holding a vast amount of historical material (an archives or a museum or a similar entity) wishes to digitize its holdings to make them available to virtual visitors from all over the world. Skills would be needed from subject matter experts (what is this item and what do we need to tell the audience about it?), from indexers (how can we tag the digital record representing it for maximum findability no matter what the age and knowledge level of the browsing individual?), from information technology experts (what kind of repository and search engine is best suited?), from digitization experts (what is the best option for creating a virtual representation of the item—in view of potential fragility and many other considerations?), and from marketing professionals (how do we entice millions of visitors to spend time in our virtual treasure trove?). Senior executives would know to call on such a range of professionals if they had in fact had exposure through their working lives to professions adjacent to their own.

►►► *WHAT DO YOU THINK, WILLIAM AND LISA?*

William and Lisa are second-year students in a graduate information program.

Lisa: I applied to the Faculty of Information Studies because a few friends of mine had inspired me through telling me about the program. It never entered my mind to think about societal status—other than to be reassured that, like school teachers and nurses, librarians generally are viewed with respect. Oh, mind you, now that I think of it, teachers and nurses are indispensable ... I get it now! But really, my motivation for choosing that program was my sense that it was a good match to my personal intellectual interests. It seemed a good extension to my undergraduate degree in sociology.

William: My reaction is similar. I actually have it in the family—my dad is a librarian at a technical vocational college. I grew up feeling comfortable in the environment and felt it was a very honorable way to make a living. I don't know that I would be too worried about having "societal clout" as you put it. I want to eventually provide for my family doing something I actually enjoy, and I'm already enjoying my part time student assistant job.

Your reactions are typical, and understandable. I would not have expected you to tell me you gauged your choice of graduate studies against an "influence-o-meter."

For you, William—assuming you do proceed to a series of positions within academic libraries—the prospects are good that you will enjoy your career. That said, you may want to pay close attention to the foreseeable challenges in academic librarianship—budget constraints and the new ways of managing the teaching and learning process being just two. You could find yourself spending a lot of time on justifying your position and those of your colleagues as opposed to collaborating with faculty on curriculum support, or you could find yourself deep in the weeds of license terms in protracted negotiations with

(Cont'd)

---

content vendors as opposed to spending time with students. It could not hurt immersing yourself in the professional discussions about return on investment, for example. I would urge you to build as many connections as you can in the community of individuals who ultimately control the budgets of academic institutions—that would be politicians—and in the community of individuals who impact public opinion about education—that could include journalists and media types. They benefit from hearing directly from you and your colleagues in the trenches about the value of quality information support in educational institutions.

For you, Lisa, I'm curious what sort of work you envision yourself doing?

Lisa: I'm hoping to combine my interest in community services and urban revitalization with my interest in information management—I'm not sure exactly how!

It's a good thing we are librarians! You are in a position, already now, to look into the kinds of agencies typically engaged in community services and make a little descriptive inventory to decide which ones appeal to you more. It would be fair to say they are up against a number of challenges calling for them to be able to impact public opinion or donor sentiment in the case of nonprofits. Your connections, too, will be important as the kind of agency you may end up working for will certainly benefit from positive media coverage and social media discussions.

Do you see how influence and positive public attention—whether it comes from you individually or from the company you keep in terms of your networks—would in fact be a benefit in your careers?

William: I had never looked at it that way ... but in fact, my dad has been saying that it's no longer enough to be a good college librarian because the old academic models are changing. I'll need to talk to him some more about that.

Lisa: I can see how being an engaged professional means taking part in events and groups and "movements" going well beyond one's actual job. It would be hard to build the kind of networks

(Cont'd)

you are talking about by just focusing on the day to day work. Being a professional is all about devoting time over and above office hours. I never thought about those implications ... but I realize the rewards of a career don't come without investment of effort. I see that I must join all the urban renewal groups. I could start by chatting up my brother's urban gardening group!

Right on the money. Lisa, it would be important to be a member of the community groups and associations working in the areas you care about—maybe small business entrepreneurship or youth programs—so that you can feed information from them into your own actual work and so you can keep them informed about your challenges and about the support your organization needs. William, you may want to be sure you belong to—or at least follow—the professional groups the college graduates will eventually join. That way you will have your ear to the ground as to the trends in the industries in question, and you may be able to solicit support from future employers when it comes to advocating for library budgets and for your and your colleagues' role at the college.

William: And aren't I lucky that I have someone right in my own family who can in fact introduce me around to these groups you speak about!

You get it ... let me just encourage you that although it sounds like a lot of effort to schmooze with all these groups of people, it will pay off. One good way to begin building your networks is to offer something—perhaps blog posts or tweets or even an informal current awareness service—relevant to the work of the group. When you arrive with something in hand, it facilitates the conversation. Lisa, if you don't happen to know a leading figure in your target networks already, you might consider finding the people who could introduce you to individuals who may have published in the field or have been featured in the media. My bottom line for you is never to hesitate investing in this schmoozing work. You know what the sportswear manufacturer says: Just do it!

Who is in charge of our image? Professional reputation management

In this chapter, we discuss our options for managing the impressions others, especially potential employers, have of us.

2.1 Who are we? Career identities, brands, and elevator speeches

"Who are we—and who do we want and need to be in future—to our direct clients and employers, to those who may be impacted indirectly by what we do, and to our peers?" On one occasion, for the purposes of an upcoming presentation, I took the liberty of asking a couple of colleagues for a reality check: What is the "brand" that comes to mind when you think of my work as an information professional? Much to my relief, the answers in part corresponded to what I had hoped to hear and in part surprised me positively. It turns out to be a common experience that what we take for granted in our skills inventory stands out for others.

Before we communicate about our services to various stakeholder groups, we may want to establish what perceptions already exist about the function and the role we have. We are likely to find a wide range of impressions depending on the interaction we may have had with any respondent or depending on the experience he or she may have had with other information professionals—and it would be surprising if some of those impressions didn't differ from what we ourselves thought. Brands are powerful carriers of connotation for products, services, and organizations—in building ours, we want to make sure it's the right one. Are we brilliant miracle makers pulling chestnuts out of fires … or steady, dependable planners who always anticipate a future need? Are we leading edge technology wizards obviously suitable for that new tech project … or experienced defusers of apprehension in a project? Are we fast workers who can pull together vast amounts of data into a tightly produced visualization … or patient diggers who can get to the bottom of system malfunction baffling the technical team? You get the idea: What mental imagery do you want for your constituents to see when they think of you or your team?

Yes, the exercise may at first appear to have some tinge of the "how much are we admired on a scale from 1 to 10" rating I always caution against—but that is handled by focusing on the role, not on ourselves as persons. Crafting the work-related brand we want to have vis-a-vis our various stakeholder groups is a challenge for many reasons familiar to information professionals. For us, it's imperative to work effectively with our clients in ways they find directly and strategically beneficial. We may never have the opportunity to share how much effort was involved in the enabling work we perform in order to deliver stunning results very quickly from time to time; that is a conversation for another day.

The title of the theme song for the original TV series *CSI* (*Crime Scene Investigation*) is "Who are you?" I "hear" it every time I think about how our professional roles are perceived. We could all benefit from a bit of investigative digging now and then: *We* know who we are ... but what brand do we really have in the eyes of those we strive to serve?

Of course, we are likely to assume different brands as we mature in our careers, transition to serving different groups of stakeholders, and take on management roles. What is important is to be aware that "perception is reality" and that *how we are seen* by the clientele is a powerful determinant of our professional success.

Thinking about the brand you want to develop and project for yourself—vis-a-vis your stakeholders to entice them to engage you in their projects or among your peers to maximize the chances of being mentioned when a position becomes available—you may find it helpful to ponder your own reaction to branding as we know it from the consumer goods sphere. You may never have touched one, but you know how a Rolex or TagHeuer watch is different from a Casio or a Swatch, and you know how a MontBlanc fountain pen is different from a Bic ballpoint. (No value judgment is implied; the various products were developed for varying purposes and audiences.) Why would you know something about a product you have never touched? Because you have heard about it in advertising for years. You know to expect durability from a Samsonite suitcase and good value from a stay at a Holiday Inn because you have been told of those qualities. In that same way, it is possible to send a message to our target market (paying customers if we are consultants or freelancers and internal users if we are employees) about what they may expect from our services.

One challenge, however, is the relatively short time frame we have at our disposal—the luxury of nurturing our brands over decades is not available the way it has been, say, for some iconic manufacturers. We may have but weeks or months in which to get across our professional brand—or even seconds. Much has been said about the need to perfect an "elevator speech" distillation of what we offer—a short but engaging description intended to pique the interest of the listener. If you have attempted to craft one, you know the truth: it is insanely difficult!

Here's how I tackled it once: *It is 11 o'clock. Do you know what your knowledge workers are doing with the expensive time and resources **you** pay for? At de Stricker Associates, we help our clients understand and then set priorities as to options for knowledge management, intercollegial sharing, and corporate memory so that they spend their money and efforts wisely and with the best possible results.* Such a statement is meant for the ears of a senior executive well aware of the cost of salaries for highly educated employees; I would make a different pitch to a manager concerned about the growing inability of employees to find documents on the intranet: "*We help clarify your options for capturing and later finding your documents.*"

No matter what you do professionally, perfect your 30-second story to do justice to your brand. Come up with variations for different audiences such as the interns versus the senior leaders in the company where you work. Polish the confidence and conviction with which you speak, and have on hand anecdotes to illustrate the elements in your story in case anyone asks for more detail. Have the spiel down pat—and make sure it's focused on client/user benefits: say (as an example) "my work enables you to save time and effort, reduce risk, and reach a much larger target audience" rather than "I perform in-depth market research" or "I conduct industry studies." In advising my colleagues to speak to client advantage, I stress that *how* we are able to deliver that advantage is our concern, not the client's. In fact, let me be extra blunt on this point: if a client expresses admiration for something you did, the correct response is "always happy to help; feel free to tell your colleagues." ("Oh, it was quite simple" is NOT a comment *ever* to be uttered!)

Social capital: Invest in it

In many career related conversations, the concept of social capital comes up, reinforcing that it deserves deliberate attention. Looking back, I see how building social capital paved the way for the evolution of my own career—a key factor was an innate tendency toward assistance to colleagues and association activities over and above the responsibilities of work. Now, I am in a position to advise younger career builders: "Invest in your social capital—it will produce results, if not tomorrow, then later throughout your working life."

By social capital I mean the reputation we build as we contribute to the communities in which we move professionally and personally, and I mean the "brand" or "label" we attach to ourselves through those contributions. It involves the "bank account" of trust and rapport we draw on when we need support for an idea or outright help in a specific situation. We may not think of it as social capital building when we respond to a request with "of course I can do that for you"—but that is the cumulative outcome.

Here is a sampling of tips for social capital building:

- Sign up: Offer to perform a task or role in a relevant group or association. Even better, run for office. Serving in an official capacity looks good on the resume.
- Write up: Tell the editors of a newsletter/bulletin/blog that you will contribute a piece ... or four. Summarizing key points from a conference session may be a good beginning ... later, add pieces arising from your own professional pursuits.
- Show up: Come to the local events put on by your professional associations and speak to attendees you don't already know. In so doing you easily broaden your reach and visibility in the community.
- Link up: Use the professional networking tools to stay within reach of those who may need your skills.
- Pick up: Consciously endeavor to earn a reputation as someone who picks up the phone, the challenge, and the lead.

(Cont'd)

As those activities accumulate, they earn a rightful place on the resume. Potential employers may not think "social capital" when they read it, but they do appreciate seeing how, on top of employment achievements, job candidates volunteered their skills for the benefit of others.

2.2 Projecting the brand in the job interview: Tell the story—then practice, practice, and practice some more!

Sometimes, candidates with strong qualifications miss out on a job offer *because they aren't practiced in the art of answering difficult questions with ease.* Here are three essential recommendations I always stress in my career workshops:

1. *Practice the answers to likely questions over and over until they roll off the tongue smoothly.* During such practice, you will soon notice when a particular phrase sounds odd, when the logic is not quite right, or when a particular formulation doesn't do justice to what you have to offer. Practicing your answers boosts confidence that you won't dilute your message with ums and ahs, and it helps you retain poised composure. If a colleague or a friend is not on hand to act as interviewer, a pet or a door will do just fine!

2. *Dig out and memorize specific stories to illustrate points you want to make.* It is essential to be able to back up with concrete evidence every skill and competence we say we possess. Prepare anecdotes to tell in response to questions: "In my position with ABC, there was *X situation* and I took *Y action* to achieve *Z outcome.*" Let me illustrate the art of the considered and constructive answer, using common questions posed in job interviews:

➤ YOU HAVE HAD SEVERAL JOBS IN THE LAST 5 YEARS? (The implication could be that you bail if things get difficult, or that you were let go.)

☐ *Yes, in those years, I have probably experienced a disproportionate share of significant organizational change resulting in downsizings or outright department closures. In no case was my performance at issue, but it has indeed been challenging to deal with quite so much change beyond my control. Conversely, having made these transitions has taught me how to deal with change successfully, and I have added to my knowledge about organizational settings. I feel I have come out stronger professionally as a result.*

☐ *Yes, I did in fact realize at one point during my employment at DEF Corporation that I was not a good fit. Rather than deprive the employer of the opportunity to find someone more suited, I decided to move on. I should add that I offered to train my successor. From what I understand, it was a good decision—the new incumbent became very successful in the job.*

☐ *Yes, I was headhunted to the GHI marketing position. Not long after I arrived, management decided to outsource several functions including mine. I was then able to negotiate for the communications related position at GHI.*

➤ YOU HAVE BEEN IN THE SAME POSITION FOR 14 YEARS? (The implication could be that you lack ambition or were not material for promotions.)

☐ *Yes, it has been my privilege to serve during many years of growth and change. As I became someone with deep insight into the corporate history,*

I gradually became a go-to person for colleagues in other departments, and over the years many special projects were entrusted to me. As a result, I built my project management skills. My most recent project to digitize the corporate archives and develop an anniversary historical exhibit—in real life as well as on the intranet—was very successful. It was a benefit that I could draw on so many people's cooperation because they have known me over the years.

□ *Yes, I felt very much in my element and enjoyed teaching generations of scientists the ins and outs of navigating the literature. Over time, I became a regular partner whenever one of them was writing for publication. I managed the research and manuscript preparation and submission process for many authors, and I was given quite a few incentives to keep up that work. That said, it is now time for me to hand my functions over and apply my skills in a growing environment.*

□ *As you can see from the successive titles, I was given increasing responsibility over the years. From the earliest position of junior reference specialist, I ended up in charge of the business intelligence function. I acquired a great deal of expertise and industry knowledge from this solid progression and am now ready to work in a larger organization.*

➤ YOUR RESUME MENTIONS PLANNING SKILLS. CAN YOU GIVE MORE DETAIL? (The implication could be that the resume lacks substantiating information.)

□ *I make it a practice to look ahead and prepare to minimize future effort. As an example, in my job at JKL Company I anticipated a product launch and set up long in advance a spreadsheet showing the functions my boss would need to address; it saved a lot of time for everyone when the launch date came closer. Another example would be the conference I planned for MNO Organization. I had the privilege of handling every aspect from program content and speaker engagements to venue selection and catering to registration and logistics, and I'm proud to say the event was smoothly executed and received rave reviews from attendees.*

☐ *The uneven workloads resulting from changes in the company's services required me to prepare contingency staffing plans and budgets, usually 18–24 months in advance. It was quite a balancing act to tune the student assistants' availability according to the fluctuations, and I always attempted to provide as much stability as I could for them.*

➤ YOU INDICATE STRONG INTERPERSONAL SKILLS. COULD YOU ELABORATE? (The implication might be that it is unclear what is meant by the expression.)

☐ *In my previous work, I have encountered a number of situations you might call "tense." I have done a fair amount of reading up on strategies for dealing with teams and coworkers, and on several occasions I have been successful at resolving conflict. For example, at PQR, it hurt productivity when two colleagues disagreed on how to proceed with a project and the unpleasantness was allowed to persist. I took it upon myself to speak in depth with each party to learn the motivations for the opinions held, and I was able to forge a compromise that not only made sense operationally but also allowed each party to*

*save face. The other staff members were grateful for
my contribution to restoring a good atmosphere.*

☐ *My role required the cooperation of several other
departments that were not formally obligated to assist. By carefully nurturing the relationships with the
team leaders, I was able to establish a rapport with
them that greatly contributed to their willingness
to collaborate. I made sure to emphasize with senior management the tremendous business value we
achieved by working together. Of course, I looked
for ways to reciprocate by offering these team leaders tailored services useful to them.*

➤ TELL US ABOUT A SITUATION IN WHICH YOU DEMONSTRATED
INITIATIVE AND/OR LEADERSHIP. (The interviewers are attempting to gauge not only your proactive skills but
also how you present them.)

☐ *In casual conversation with employees, it emerged
there was an interest in learning more about trends
in the industry. I set up a lunch-and-learn lecture series and recruited speakers to share their expertise.
The lectures were extremely popular, and the concept was in fact copied in other departments. To help
attendees with their annual performance reviews, I
made sure to issue "attendance certificates" so that
they could document the topics they had learned
about.*

☐ *When I added a new tool to the intranet suite, it
became clear that I had underestimated the appetite
among users for it **and** its complexity. I quickly put
together a brief guide and used my excellent relationship with the webmaster to get it posted prom-
inently on the splash page. In addition, I scheduled*

a series of lunchtime visits to the business teams so that I could demonstrate the tool and answer questions. I received a lot of positive feedback as a result, and usage statistics went through the roof as in fact the resource was extremely relevant to the business teams. The experience taught me that pilots are a valuable tool in introducing new tools.

3. **Prepare questions to ask the interviewers about the organization and the position.** Doing so signals that you have taken the time to become oriented about the likely needs of the organization and that you are truly focused on delivering value to it. Have up your sleeve, for the portion when you are typically given the opportunity to ask questions, such queries as:

➤ HOW DO YOU FORESEE INDUSTRY DEVELOPMENTS IMPACTING THE ORGANIZATION IN THE NEXT 12–18 MONTHS? (The question shows you keep your antennae out and gives the interviewers a chance to share their perceptions, thus allowing you to get a sense how they use their answers as selling points for the position.)

➤ ARE THERE STRATEGIC PLANS OR INITIATIVES UNDER WAY THAT COULD BE RELEVANT FOR THE POSITION? (The question shows you are a big-picture thinker and further provides for you to gauge how the interviewers see the position's fit with the overall direction of the organization.)

➤ HOW WOULD YOU CHARACTERIZE THE CULTURE IN THE DEPARTMENT, FOR EXAMPLE IN TERMS OF THE APPETITE FOR INNOVATION? (The question positions you as a forward planner and innovator and gives the interviewers an opportunity to provide yet another positive feature about the organization.)

Certainly you will be anxious to find out "when will the decision be made," but such a question is best left to the very end when you have demonstrated that you have thought about the position and researched the organization and the industry.

2.3 Negotiate from a position of honesty: That's just part of the brand

Among the many tips readily available for making a positive impression in an interview, these two are at the top of my list:

1. *The best approach is to be genuine, heeding "truth in advertising" advice.* Of course we all wish to present favorably, but being candid is likely to help us feel more relaxed and to give interviewers a better impression. For example, if you feel saying "I have experience with ..." is a stretch, you may be more comfortable saying "I have had exposure to ...". In advance, speak out loud to the refrigerator the various possible statements you could make—your gut will tell you which one is right.

2. *The interview is a trade negotiation.* We want the job, and the employer wants the best candidate. Hence we compete with other applicants for a position—and the employers compete for the most suitable applicants. Go in from a position of strength, thinking "just as you want to discover whether you should invest in me, I'm here to find out if the job would be a good career move for me." You are entitled to ask questions about the organization's culture!

There is no shortage of information resources to support job seekers—yet no amount of advice has the impact practice has. Sure it feels weird talking to the walls at first … but trust me, the effort will be worth the time!

2.4 As you start a new job: Brand yourself from the beginning

As workplaces undergo considerable change in these times, it is more than ever essential for new graduates without previous full time work experience to be prepared for the norms and expectations characteristic of organizational cultures; for that reason I emphasize the "soft skills" topic whenever I speak about careers. Usually triggered by the question "should courses and grades be on one's resume?", our conversation focuses on the simple but stunning fact—in the context of the work load in graduate school—that supervisors and coworkers rarely care about academic achievements. Instead, they care greatly about skills in adapting to the needs of the workplace, working on teams, dealing with clients, representing the employer professionally, and so on. In addition, let me suggest:

- Read up on the industry or sector in question: what developments are having an impact on the work of organizations like the one you will be joining, and what challenges could therefore be expected?

- Find out as much as you can about your new employer: Use your research skills to shed light on the past and likely future of the specific environment where you will be working.

- Brush up on the key elements of emotional intelligence and interpersonal communication; you will need considerable social nimbleness given the work relationships likely to exist in your new group of colleagues.

- Lean on colleagues who have gone before you: what did the graduates from a few years ago learn as they started their first jobs? What could seasoned colleagues tell you? (Oh, and you know where to find these colleagues—in the relevant professional association.)

- Finally, don't be afraid to ask questions of your new boss and new team! Asking shows you are interested in performing well and acting appropriately, and it's better to ask than to assume and be off the mark.

How's this for a brand: Musician in the organizational orchestra

At a concert, I had the opportunity to watch at close range the intricate workings of the orchestra supporting opera singers. The musicians worked the piano, strings, and percussion—what an amazing array of drums, cymbals, hanging xylophones, rainstick-type instruments, and other sound producing objects I don't even know how to name!—to organize and sequence thousands of individual notes into a harmonious, powerful, and sometimes surprising result. The light manager provided a splendid visual complement to the music, and the copious amounts of water vapor released into the concert hall lent a touch of magic. Each song performed reached back through decades or centuries to revered composers and was given life in the moment by the latest technology—in a manner uniquely suited to the occasion and the audience.

Giving thought to the vast planning and coordination required to produce an experience so clearly enjoyed by the sold-out house, it struck me: Isn't that what information professionals do, too? Don't we "orchestrate" myriad individual preparatory and immediate actions in order to "produce" the experience our audiences receive? Don't we collaborate within our organizations and across the profession to gain the skills to, well, play those

(Cont'd)

---

instruments with such perfect timing? Don't we rely on the work done in decades and centuries before us and on the latest technology to meet our clients' unique needs? Don't we plan and organize so that the "star performers"—our users—get to deliver outstanding results? As for the tenors ... they, too, seemed like information professionals to me, bringing to bear their education and talent on producing value. We're talking world class operatic stars who related to the audience with humility, warm humor, and personable ease. In just that way I so often see information professionals being utterly modest and unassuming about their work, no matter how outstanding it is. Don't they deliver spectacular performances in the way they hit just the right notes when they do research or produce strategic plans?

Indeed, we information professionals do not actually perform in misty, colored lights on a background of exquisite music to deliver value to our clients. But in my humble opinion, we are pretty close.

►►► *WHAT DO YOU THINK, GHEETA AND DANIEL?*

Gheeta graduated two years ago and now works in a pension fund. Daniel graduated four years ago and now works in the IT department of medium-sized firm.

Daniel: I guess my considerable technical skills constituted a kind of brand when I was fresh out of school ... though I did not think of it that way. I landed a job here at the company because a friend put in a good word with the IT manager in charge of the website; there was a huge rebuild coming, and the projects I had done in the last semester impressed the team. So I had my marching orders and got very busy immediately. Since then, I have been on several development tasks with a small group of colleagues, and now that you mention it, I believe I did begin to

(Cont'd)

project a brand. It seems I have a knack for designing positive customer experience, and that is highly valued here.

Gheeta: Like Daniel, I couldn't say I had a brand when I applied for my job—but thinking back now, I see that I had some strong relevant subject background on my resume, and then I did a really good job in the interview. In fact I was told that my ability to field those tough questions with confidence was a key factor in my getting the job. As you can imagine, the environment here is pretty intense—after all, we manage the money that is going to pay the pensions for all those thousands of contributors one day. I handle the news and industry monitoring and feed the intranet, and I respond to requests for special deep-dive research when that is required. No, I didn't consciously focus on branding myself, but again like Daniel I suppose my reputation among my clients here has grown quickly. It's gratifying to hear them say things like "we know we can rely on Gheeta to come through every time," and I love it when I alert someone to an item I noticed and get back a reply like "how could you know I needed to see that—you saved my bacon!".

It sounds as if you have each instinctively built a reputation for quality and talent by hard work and attention to the preferences of customers and the needs of colleagues in the enterprise. I assume you feel quite secure in your positions?

Gheeta: Yes, and I'm guessing where you are going with this. Will it be sufficient over the longer term for us to keep doing a good job?

Daniel: Right, at my last performance review there was that typical question "where do you see yourself in X years" and I did not have a clear answer.

You are in a wonderful position now, from where you are, to begin plotting your future paths and building your brands to match and support the jobs you will hold as time goes on. You are popular with your colleagues; now you may want to think through how you are perceived by your peer community as well. Maybe one day a really attractive opportunity will show up at another organization.

(Cont'd)

Daniel: Yes, I see what you mean. I have lots to keep me occupied for right now, but I can't just keep doing one project after another—that would stop being fulfilling. So either I aim for more responsibility where I am, or keep an open mind for moving on. The question is whether I want to keep my hands in the technical weeds or progress to management roles, I guess?

Gheeta: I could see using my reputation as a springboard into some of the knowledge management initiatives going on. I have had a few conversations with my happy clients about those initiatives, and I casually offered that of course, KM is well within my professional field. I could see the wheels turning in their heads when I said that.

You are on the right track. Sure, for a time you enjoy succeeding at what you do, but the world does not stand still. So yes Daniel, you would want to have that talk with your boss about opportunities for you to take on project leadership—as opposed to being the technical wizard on the team. That could imply the need for reading up on project management—better yet, take a course unless your firm provides such training. That would give you a taste of management and tell you whether you are just as skilled at and interested in it as you are skilled at and interested in technical design. And yes Gheeta, I would absolutely encourage you to bone up on KM and expand those conversations you already have had. Perhaps you could ask to be attached to a KM project team as an information liaison and use that role as a means of getting started working on KM at the fund.

Gheeta: What you are saying, I think, is that we begin now to expand our brands beyond the excellence we are already known for. I can see how, if I were to attend the local KM meetups, I could get to know the "KM stars" in town. Couldn't hurt my future opportunities to find out more about what these people do and to learn about the types of projects they are involved in—not to mention, over time of course, impressing them just as I have impressed my clients at work.

Daniel: Hm, you have given me something to think about. Qualifications in project management are definitely going to be

(Cont'd)

viewed positively in the firm, and I confess to being intrigued by the thought of one day managing large scale IT projects. I'm getting the notion of what you mean by expanding the professional brand. For starters, I'll accept the invitation my boss sent out for the next meeting of the web developers' club downtown. Who knows where it could lead?

I made my case ...

3

Why should we serve? The value of (volunteering in) professional associations

In this chapter, we discuss the role of professional associations in our careers. Information professionals well into their work lives may have had personal experience to convince them of the value inherent in at least belonging to, but ideally serving in, professional associations. Students and recent graduates may not be privy to such insight. Therefore, I bring up the topic now, early in our conversation about your career.

3.1 Our professional connections are powerful assets for employers

My ardent belief in the value of professional associations is no secret, and I support my comments by serving on boards of directors, on committees, and in special assignments. As a result of many active roles held over the decades, I have experienced how valuable it is to be but a message away from having doors opened, getting crucial contacts established, and so on.

Over and above formal continuing education, our colleagues' willingness to support fellow professionals is gold when it comes to bolstering our skills. The luxury of garnering input from fellow association members is a key to our ability to grow as professionals as we solve day to day challenges. But there's more: our professional connections are assets to our employers—not just bullet points on our resumes—and should be promoted as such.

Of course, our direct clients benefit when we leverage connections on their behalf—for example, when we zero in on unique content in a matter of minutes via the guidance of our peers. In a more general way, our employers benefit when we can build on the professional connections made at last month's conference or during years of service in an association—for example, as we use our peers' insight and experience, shared at meetings and on discussion lists, to inform the activities we undertake.

When expenses and time associated with conference or meeting attendance are legitimately under scrutiny, it is important to build the business case why *the investment we make in building professional networks is very much worthwhile*: That investment—our contributions in return for the takeaways—is our means of gaining admission to the combined expertise of our professional networks ... for the good of the work we do. The specific business advantage of our collegial networks deserves being featured clearly in our official resumes and social profiles. If we have previously taken networking activities for granted (as in "yes of course I have served in leadership roles in professional groups"), it may be time to articulate explicitly the positive results arising for our employers and clients. The annual performance review could be a good regular occasion—but why not take the opportunity whenever it arises?

3.2 Investing in our careers: Conferences are not a luxury

Rave reviews from conference attendees are a perfect case study illustrating the value of direct interaction between peers with similar interests and concerns. Enthusiastic feedback to the organizing team may focus on the long range benefits and takeaways of discovering the latest thinking in relevant topical areas, having confidence-building "aha" moments, and establishing personal contacts. The typical conversation among attendees about the value of any given conference reflects comments I have heard throughout my working life.

Given the understandable personal budgetary concerns, I want to stress the salient and universally applicable points regarding personal investment of time and money in professional conferences. Unless it just so happens a conference is held in our back yard, the out of pocket costs—shared car rides and hotel rooms notwithstanding—are significant. But I believe they are *necessary and justifiable* investments:

- Hearing what speakers have to say and what fellow attendees think about it right then and there is a nuanced experience offering the opportunity to ask face to face "could you give an example?", "how did you specifically implement?", "what should I be concerned about given my situation?", and so on. The value of shaking the hand of a speaker—who, by definition, would be a respected and knowledgeable individual—should not be underestimated in the context of building professional relationships. (Sending a personal note of appreciation subsequently couldn't hurt.)

- The personal connections we make at a conference may last—and yield yet more connections—for our entire careers.

- The value of the trust arising from having interacted personally cannot be overstated.

- The concentrated dose of information we may obtain from colleagues would likely be much more time consuming to obtain via websites, social media, podcasts, etc.

- Where there are exhibits, the conference is a unique opportunity for everyone to learn about information industry trends and for buyers to engage with vendors in detailed discussions about their products and services.

- Demonstrations and brief tutorials are typically offered on the spot.

- Viewed over the long career term, what we pay to be with our peers at a professional conference is worth every bit of the investment. Of course, we arrive with detailed agendas outlining how to spend the precious hours soaking up the program offerings. Then, using the social events to catch up with colleagues and meet new ones is a valuable bonus—requiring, of course, some stamina on top of a 10-hour day packed with activities.

Having benefited from and enjoyed (and yes, returned exhausted from) professional conferences for decades, it is second nature for me to prioritize them in my budgeting. I encourage every information professional to develop and maintain the habit: invest in your career—go join your peers!

3.3 Use the hallways—They are more productive than they look

The fact that "schmoozing" can be a powerful means of building networks is well known—yet some colleagues tell me they are uncomfortable approaching and chatting up people "just like that." Let me share some compelling evidence I hope will encourage even those who think of themselves as introverts to be deliberate about reaching out to others. Surprising results could ensue for your projects, initiatives, and teams.

It is my life long experience that at a professional event, no one is a stranger and no one objects to being approached. In the days of traversing the conference venues, I met scores of new colleagues—some for a few moments, others for lengthy in-depth discussions ... just by saying hello. Cards were exchanged, further connections made (I'll put you in touch with so-and-so), and astonishing coincidences with significant implications were discovered. Several chance encounters ended with "I'm *so glad* we had this conversation," and a few times I finally encountered in person someone well known to me from his or her publications.

Of course, well-established professionals make a point of introducing new entrants to their colleagues, knowing from experience how much it benefits all parties. For anyone less sure how to "work the crowd," here are some suggestions for what to do in the hallways and at receptions when people are not obviously rushing or staring at their devices:

- Keep many business cards on hand. Ideally, the card should be customized to remind recipients why they have it and why they may want to connect again. For example, an annotation could read "Seeking employment in digitization projects." The back of the card can be used for a "mini resume."

- Variations of "so far, what has been the best experience for you here?" could be a good opener. It is useful to learn how colleagues perceive the event—and conference organizers appreciate the input!

- If you see someone on his or her own, walk up, stick your hand out, and be direct: "Hi, I'm Ulla from Toronto—are you enjoying the conference?" Chances are the person you approach welcomes being greeted. (In the unlikely event he or she signals a desire to be left alone, just move on.)

- You are entitled to go beyond small talk: "May I ask what you are looking for when filling a position like the one you described?"

- Look for something to offer, be it professional or personal: "Would you like me to prepare a brief usability critique of your website?" or "I'll be happy to suggest great places to visit in Toronto that aren't in the guidebooks."

3.4 More on schmoozing: Value for the conference dollar

When a colleague commented "isn't it amazing how people at conferences spend their time gazing at a screen?", the memory of making an international connection was germane. At one conference, I spoke to a stranger across the lunch table who did not seem to know those around her. A few sentences later, I knew just who among my colleagues she needed to meet and wasted no time getting that to happen! As I headed for the airport, I spotted the two of them in the coffee shop, deep in conversation. How else could this US-European connection have been made? (Postscript: My lunch table companion did subsequently issue a consulting contract to my colleague.)

Every minute spent NOT getting to know new people at a conference is a precious opportunity lost.

3.5 When conference season is upon us ...

Large numbers of information professionals head off to conferences during the summer—yours truly included. For everyone, the conference is a welcome annual professional highlight. For those attending, being at the sessions, visiting exhibitors, and seeing to the social networks is serious work! For those engaged in arranging sessions, the conference may be a culmination of up to 18 months of work. That is where volunteering truly pays off: What could be more gratifying than to prepare a valuable experience for colleagues?

Every association needs willing hands to make events happen, get out the newsletter, take care of the website and blogs, and scout for members deserving of special recognition ... not to mention stand for election to the board of directors. There is a need for every volunteer ... and do consider that association roles and positions look good on a resume.

Professional associations are an invaluable source of collegial support and inspiration—in fact, many say the number one reason they are members is the networking benefit. But associations don't run themselves. Of course, many may hesitate to add volunteer commitments to already crowded schedules. That is understandable ... yet let's keep in mind that active participation is an investment in ourselves and in our careers.

If you are not sure what role is most appropriate for you, a phone call to the volunteer coordinator or to a member of the board of directors will show the way. Just do it—who knows what professional opportunities may ensue?

So ... when you think of volunteering, conference or webinar activities may appeal to you because they are so highly associated with value for members. No matter what—say, handling event registrations—just take it from there.

3.6 Speaking of volunteering: A sharing of the wealth

It is a worrying concern for habitual conference goers—not to mention presenters—that overall, employer funding for professional events and training appears under pressure, limiting opportunities for some to interact in person with their colleagues across the world.

The benefit of professional growth and value brought back to employer organizations in the form of new skills may not sway budget managers, and taking vacation days and footing personally the entire bill for attending a major conference may not be feasible.

If the cost of in-person participation in an event in a major city is prohibitive, it is especially important for us to get the most out of local or virtual networking, asking questions, discovering how others have tackled a challenge, and so on. It is essential to reach out and share the wealth—the wealth of what we know and what we have to offer—with our colleagues. If you haven't already done so, now is a good time to enhance that profile on social media and to become an active contributor of comments to relevant blogs or to create a personal blog.

Giving to professional communities is a spectacularly effective means of achieving career-enhancing visibility without cringing. Don't hesitate, just get started!

3.7 Volunteer: It's your career

For those who may be counseling new professionals, a brief review of "what's not to love about volunteering" is offered here:

- You will have someone to guide you—say, a previous committee chair or a unit leader. But if you don't for any reason—you have the freedom to move in new directions!

- You get to tackle typical or unforeseen projects and demonstrate your skill.

- You get to be in front of potential future employers and of people who can put in a good word as references.

- You get to demonstrate your competence comfortably until you are ready to take on a solo role. Serving on a committee before you take on chairing one is a good way to begin.

- You get to put your accomplishments on your resume.

Volunteering is a stellar opportunity to grow professionally and to gain visibility. Indeed, what is not to love?

Ah, you may think. But what if I don't do well? It would be quite the risk to embarrass myself in front of peers! That is where collegial collaboration comes in. It is perfectly appropriate to ask a colleague for a bit of guidance or showing-of-the-ropes, at least in the beginning. Moreover, there is usually a high level of tolerance in volunteer environments; it is understood that there's a first time for everything, and the attitude of support prevails.

Indeed, volunteering has two sides: Doing it ... and enticing others to do it. For those who have already volunteered in many roles, the next step is encouraging others to follow suit and to ensure they grow comfortably with the new role.

3.8 Help others volunteer: That, too, helps your career

Experienced volunteers sometimes comment how they struggle with what they perceive as excessive modesty on the part of younger colleagues or recent graduates (who may not be younger but who have less time in the information profession). These experienced volunteers may understandably have forgotten any hesitation *they* had when they started out.

The hesitation to volunteer may stem from nothing more than deep respect for established colleagues (as in, "oh, I could never take on a committee role next to Cecilia who has so much experience!"). It is worth finding out from the potential volunteer why he or she may be reluctant so as to address the specific reasons and provide appropriate encouragement.

For example, the potential volunteer may welcome the offer of a shadow or "co-" position on a committee or working group: "Why don't we jointly hold the role of program committee chair? We will work together to develop the lunch lecture series, and we could take turns introducing the sessions and thanking the speakers." I have seen such pairings work extremely well in practice and encourage much wider use of it.

3.9 Sharing professional expertise— It's what we do (no matter how)

Professionals have always had various means of giving others the opportunity to benefit from accumulated expertise— in books, articles, and lectures. Today's tools have given us a significant communications lift in the form of webinars: Presenters and listeners, in the comfort and convenience of their own offices, meet online to discuss matters of mutual concern at much shorter notice than would be possible for in-person events.

It is gratifying to see how thoroughly professional associations have adopted the webinar series as an adjunct to standard meetings. Of course, the price we pay for the ease of not having to travel is the degree of distance we may feel—I, for one, feel terribly isolated when I cannot see my audience and my only companion is the timer—and the occasional frustration we may feel when software acts up. We owe many thanks to those who organize and manage online meetings; I strongly advocate for vocal appreciation of all the time and effort being invested behind the scenes before and after the actual 30 or 60 minutes of the event itself.

In that experiential context, I have come to appreciate old-fashioned conferences more than ever. Only those who make them happen—by crafting the program, organizing local events, and managing the practical logistics ranging from registration to coffee to business partner participation—fully understand the complexity of planning. Again, I draw on personal experience in saying that without dedicated teams of volunteers, the conferences we attend would be quite a lot more expensive. The volunteers' contributions enhance our opportunities to renew and form connections that in many cases become lifelong. We owe them a tremendous debt of gratitude for what they give to their colleagues.

3.10 Thinking of planning a conference? Tips from a volunteer

As a career-long association volunteer, I make it a constant practice to encourage others to offer to contribute to professional events and publications, always citing the many benefits including gaining visibility, getting to know colleagues better, and learning new skills. Volunteering truly is a matter of getting more than one gives—yes, conference planning can be fun and rewarding! Here are a few success factor illustrations I would give to other conference planners, based on the positive experience of having worked with sterling teams.

- Relying on other team members is paramount. Volunteering is not about "lone heroics"—it's about collaborating to ensure work loads are reasonable. I was so lucky to have a dynamite group with lots of experience—and doesn't it speak volumes that several members signed up to volunteer for the next year!

- No matter how carefully one plans, some things (usually ones nobody notices) will escape attention. Each such discovery is a useful tip to be applied to future situations: As a result of one such experience, I learned that it is essential to arrange for a different Master of Ceremonies to handle each new session; rather than putting the onus on one (likely very stressed) person, having multiple MCs gives several others an opportunity to be "up there" getting used to the function.

- Consider the "culture" of the association to determine how to balance organizers' desire for punctual session starts with conference attendees' desire to network. At the very least, closing the doors when the session starts is a courtesy to introducers and speakers.

- Given that Conference Chairs need to check messages just as everyone else does, having a co-chair enables taking turns "hovering over the event" and "paying attention to our lives."

- Reach out to first-time attendees in various ways ranging from a simple arranged welcome handshake and chat to a formal orientation event.

- Understand and document early on for everyone on the team the allocation of tasks. If it becomes necessary, re-allocation is relatively smooth if individual task areas are clearly described.

- Keep good documentation for the current and the next crew. Next year's team is entitled to make new decisions and depart from past practice of course, but there is huge value in knowing what the previous years' experiences were.

- If there is an association management office (whose responsibilities typically would include such crucial practicalities as venue and hotel arrangements, catering and menus, AV, signage, attendee handout printing and bags, etc.), take advantage of such an office's expertise and build a solid working relationship! If there isn't such an office, consider hiring a professional planner for key logistics and overall support—evidence suggests the total work load of a typical full blown conference at a hotel or convention center is daunting for an all-volunteer crew.

- Arrange for social events in addition to the subject-oriented events. Attendees get so much out of going on tours, having meals together, and the like.

3.11 The experts are in: Useful session models for conference planners

"Speed dating events" or "mini fairs" have become a popular means for professionals to exchange insight and experience in an organized and effective manner. The format simply involves a number of fixed elements—say, tables at which individuals or groups are stationed to provide information or offer guidance—and mobile visitors who, at timed intervals, go from one display or person to another. Dance cards may be used to ensure order.

Feedback from such sessions stresses the unique benefits of a structured format: inquirers have the opportunity to meet and hear the views of a number of individuals they may otherwise have considerable difficulty arranging to meet; the nuances of responses from multiple experts may be compared; and networking connections are established for potential followup.

A related model is the "Sages on the Spot" in which 3–5 experts take questions from the audience. Here, attendees often comment how assuring it is to hear several experts offer similar or closely aligned viewpoints and insights and how interesting it is to hear different professional angles on a given career choice or workplace related matter. Observing in such a session that "others, too, are experiencing my scenario, and there are options" is a positive takeaway.

The experience and the feedback indicate that meeting planners have a valuable tool at their disposal when they work to structure sessions with specific relevance to the interests and concerns of attendees. When association leaders are dealing with the challenge of providing conference content to justify the expense for attendees, the personalized discussion format merits consideration as a component among formal sessions. Of course, avoiding the expense of AV equipment is just a side bonus for the planners!

Standing up to serve ... and voting: Aiding the profession's future

When candidates for election to office in a professional association accept the call to stand, they are to be admired and acknowledged. Associations do not run themselves; it is essential to expend every effort to entice talent to stand for election and to support the election process well.

(Cont'd)

Professional associations in general are feeling the pinch as the economy forces members to weigh expenses for membership fees and conference attendance: The reasoning may well be something like "with so many local meetups to attend and so many gratis discussion groups on LinkedIn to visit, it is getting more difficult to justify the expense of belonging to a traditional association."

All the more reason to respect those who do belong and congratulate those who venture to become candidates for office. Whether running for local, regional, national, or international level positions, individuals stepping up to the plate are to be honored for their courage. It takes guts—and sometimes thick skin—to announce to a community of peers "I want to be your leader ... and here's what I think of the current challenges and those ahead of us." Some might in fact hesitate out of reluctance to "lose"—but let me stress that no one loses in association elections. Everyone wins because of the discussions triggered by "so, who will get your vote?" type questions.

It is true that a candidate who is familiar to more voters may have an edge because of the comfort level of voting for a known quantity; but the very act of standing for election demonstrates grit and substance. There are risks—for example, association members reasonably want to understand what candidates stand for, but ideas expressed by candidates may turn out in reality, for reasons they could not know, to be impractical. Finding the perfect pitch requires insight, care, and reflection.

The flip side of honoring those who stand up to serve is encouraging members to vote. It is said about political elections that nonvoters are not entitled to complain later; just so, professional association members have a guaranteed opportunity to make their preferences known—often through a convenient online tool needing but moments. The higher the voting rate, the better the elected candidates will be in a position to act for membership interests.

Our profession is dealing with many challenges—for starters, those related to society's understanding of practitioners' value generate lots of discussion. We need the collective forces of our

(Cont'd)

associations to create attractive career prospects for members and deliver an overall positive impact on society. If the current year is not the time for any one individual to stand up as a candidate for office, then consider next year (and watch carefully what the leaders are doing in the meantime). No matter what ... vote, and ask fellow members to vote!

►►► WHAT DO YOU THINK, PAUL AND CHARLOTTE?

Paul is a law firm librarian working half of his time on KM projects with the partners and IT. Charlotte is a self-employed researcher and project manager for clients who appreciate having flexible access to her skills when required.

Charlotte: I always enjoy attending the meetings and webinars offered by my association, and the network is priceless. I'm slightly guilty that I haven't yet volunteered to serve on a committee. It's a matter of finding the time, and I wonder if I'd actually be any good.

Paul: Same here, though one of my best friends always talks about how she loves her activities in her association—she's actually on the board of directors. I ought to take her up on her offer to get me started—I'm just not sure what I could do.

Let me ask: Paul, when the law firm partners and IT personnel give you a task or ask your advice, do you excuse yourself? Charlotte, when a client requests your services, do you decline the engagement? Of course not! You are confident professionals with solid track records. Sure, you may need to orient yourself as to the specifics of any new project, but deep down you have no doubts about your capabilities. Now, can you imagine any task, role, or project in a professional association that would be beyond your abilities?

Paul: When you put it like that ... I see your point. I suppose I could tell my friend how much time I'm able to offer?

(Cont'd)

Charlotte: How much time would it in fact be typical to need to commit?

Glad I have piqued your interest that far. Let me tell you, you will be warmly received no matter what amount of time you indicate you can provide. Now, do you have any thoughts about what type of activity you might like to volunteer for?

Charlotte: I'm particularly pleased with the webinars the association offers. It would make sense for me to offer to help with the series. Not saying I could **give** a webinar—at least I'd have to think about it—but I'm sure there is quite the back and forth ahead of time with planning the topics, recruiting the speakers, writing the announcements, handling registrations, and so on. I could get in touch with the person who is currently issuing the webinar invitations and let him know that I'm interested in lending a hand.

Paul: I'm actually open to just about anything, and I recall my friend talking about how it was getting harder to get and keep volunteers because everyone is so busy these days. She mentioned something about wanting to put on a special series of meetings featuring KM topics, and I know people who would be great for speaking in such a series.

See, that was easy. You will be popular when you do reach out. Let me give you an idea what to expect—I have been around this block many times. You are probably wondering if volunteering means doing something every day and wondering how the work actually gets done in a committee. Typically, the person in charge—it sounds as if there's a webinar committee chair Charlotte and an educational programs planning role Paul— gathers the team to brainstorm about the nature of the program or series. In such a brainstorming session, it's natural to allocate the tasks—you're on content, you reach out to speakers and get their bios, you handle publicity, you handle the logistics of software or venues, and you handle registrations. The more hands, the more manageable the tasks. Some committees like to do their work in a wiki or other shared document space, others find email to be just fine. There will be drafting of event

(Cont'd)

schedules and finalization of each event description going back and forth until they are ready for publication. One or two people usually hold the keys—to the administrative webinar software or to the physical venue operators—and thus ensure the event can take place in reality. During a webinar, another person may act as the moderator, introducing the speaker and ensuring audience questions get to the speaker. In a physical event, someone needs to arrive early, ensure the room is set up properly, check on the arrival of any refreshments, and be up at the podium to welcome the audience and get the meeting started. No one of these tasks is hugely time consuming.

Charlotte: Being self-employed, my time is flexible. What about Paul—can he do association work during the work day?

Excellent question, and the answer of course depends on the law firm's culture. I doubt there'd be any problem with Paul taking care of a few emails during lunch hour, and there's always the option of spending some evening or weekend time. A few hours here and there should do it, over and above the event itself of course.

Paul: I was thinking, too, that it might actually be fun to make something happen and to work with people outside the job.

That's just it—you are likely to find the process enjoyable, and certainly it is satisfying when attendees at a program express their appreciation—be that for the great speaker, the excellent venue, the good snacks, or the smooth management of the event. At the end of a season, you should expect to have developed good relationships with the other people on the committee—relationships that will last for a long time beyond the actual time you spend on it. There will a considerable favor bank on which to draw for years to come. Have fun!

Part Two

If The Work Does Not Find Us
... We Must Find The Work

4

Venturing outside: Broadening our scope of work

I often point out that "career planning" may be a contradiction in terms, given how many of us can tell the story of falling into a particular job through happenstance and then building an entire career on that basis—but nothing stops anyone from giving luck a little push by greatly broadening the scope of the search for a job. In this chapter, we discuss the opportunities available outside the boundaries of what LIS graduates might have considered their target when they first entered graduate school.

4.1 Career transitions: More common than we thought

It is a common theme at professional conferences that career transitions are becoming more frequent. Prompted by changes in the marketplace or by personal interest or both, the career refocusing reflects a range of individual situations all sharing the common thread of adaptation to evolving conditions and interests. Especially noteworthy is the common pattern that past knowledge and expertise are indeed transferable to new endeavors: Skills in business and competitive intelligence are applicable to any new service offering; a business focusing on one type of services can add new ones; and a personal interest can become a professional focus. No matter what our original education, our past experience can be repurposed. Our customer focus stands us in good stead no matter what, and our familiarity with information management puts us in a position to undertake new projects we never could have imagined.

For many years now, we have discussed among ourselves how information professionals bring value to bear on a multitude of business challenges; the sticking point in the conversations was often "just how do we sell our skills into a business segment not customarily familiar with our offerings?" Here are some key points to ponder and use:

- We know how to identify the best sources of new knowledge and skills we want to add to our repertoires.

- We are adept at assessing trends and potential market receptivity.

- We have honed our skills in creating business cases and benefits-based proposals.

- We understand the motivations of clients in devoting time or money to acquiring a product or service.

- Our client service and communication skills are well developed.

Whether a mid-career change occurs as a result of a sudden confluence of events or as a series of smaller gradual adjustments, we all benefit from applying to our own situations the principle that the past may inform, but need not determine, our professional future.

4.2 The relevance of information credentials

It is no surprise that "information credentials" prepare professionals for many jobs and functions going far beyond the traditional ones. We know how expertise in the management of records, documents, images, multimedia clips, etc. can be applied anywhere in an organization. We know that management of intellectual property rights is a concern in many quarters. Other variations of information and knowledge expertise are relevant in workplaces that are likely outside the job search scope for recent MIS graduates and mid-to-late career changers alike—and similarly out of view for managers looking for qualified personnel. We see a need for efforts to bring together the cadre of employers needing information professionals, but not labeling them as such, and the cadre of information professionals whose skills are easily transferable to a wide range of settings.

As an example, some information professionals work as business analysts. Wouldn't information credentials be relevant in facets of safety and security work as well? Public policy analysis and development deserves a closer look as a career path for information professionals; information forensics could prove a fascinating line of work, and so on.

However, "we're not there yet." For starters, typical job descriptions, classifications, and assessments require tuning to accommodate the contributions skilled information professionals are in reality able to bring to the table. It remains a challenge for information credential holders to communicate to potential employers their relevance.

4.3 Translation from info lingo to business speak: Key task for job seekers

In many settings, information professionals discuss the theme of "salesmanship" or "crafting compelling arguments for investments, initiatives, or hiring"—especially in fields outside the core domains of libraries and archives. Employment opportunities do exist—but we must connect the dots for the potential employers. In my work, I encounter many individuals who have positions focusing heavily on knowledge acquisition, sharing, and analysis—and I always think "ah, such work would be just the ticket for an information professional." The hitch is that managers in organizations with openings whose job titles include such words as "analyst" or "officer" may be unaware how closely the LIS graduates' skill sets match the demands of the job. We can, and should, do whatever we can to raise awareness generally about the versatility of LIS qualifications.

One suggestion I give job seekers is to examine job postings broadly to identify ones using language suggesting they are "information centric" and then to apply using the business terminology appropriate for the hiring organization. Easier said than done, of course—but what's to lose? The exercise of stating our skills, past work, and accomplishments in terms meaningful for the hiring teams can only help us get better at convincing potential employers we have what it takes to be highly productive in countless environments. As examples, consider how much public policy or administration, client relations, and fund raising have in common as a result of their reliance on information and knowledge management—and then consider how pervasive intensive work with data is in business and public sector settings. Of course, any information professional could benefit from thinking about enhancing his or her technical skills—but let's not overlook the opportunities available right now among organizations looking for talented employees.

80s Eyeglasses? The unthinkable is suddenly thinkable

Imagine, those cover-half-the-face eyeglass frames we used to wear in the 80s are once again seen in trend setting fashion circles. (Was the fad of the wide temples, cutting off peripheral vision, over so soon?) Well, let's not forget that the larger the frame, the better it handles progressive lenses with triple corrections ... how's that for a consideration we never had back then! The unthinkable becoming thinkable may take us by surprise now and then. But it shouldn't. In fashion, as in our work lives, we are prepared for the strangest things when it comes to new work practices on the part of our clients, new expectations in terms of how we communicate with them, new demands for corporate strategies in knowledge support, and so on. A re-reading of Malcolm Gladwell's *The Tipping Point* reinforced the impression of the need for us to be constantly on the alert for small and subtle signs how things are changing—so that we may be ready, turning on a dime, to work with clients whose work styles have evolved or are evolving to be very different from what we were accustomed to in the past. Then again: Certainly we are prepared to accommodate "thumb generation" preferences for dealing with information through evolving always-on mobile tools—but what do we then make of articles written by individuals who cut themselves off from 24/7 connectivity, at least for a time, in an effort to preserve sanity? Old fashioned information packages in print to be read at leisure, anyone? As time rolls on, our profession is learning that multiple and sometimes opposite changes happen quickly. We roll on too, and embrace the old and the new, and the old *as the new*, as the case may be.

4.4 Bottom line: We are all in business

I always encourage information professionals to watch what the self-employed are "up to" ... for a simple reason: In my view we are all in the *business* of earning our clients' and investors' attention, engagement, and support. Public libraries must prove their value to the community, special libraries must demonstrate to funders that they are worth the cost, intranet managers must demonstrate their work pays off for the organization, and so on. We must communicate in ways to stimulate the interest and attention of our target audiences ... just the way any other business must. In my talks and workshops, I express that view pointedly by asking "what would you say if you were asked why the salaries you and your colleagues earn are worth it to the employer?" and "complete the sentence beginning with YOU PAY ME BECAUSE YOU WANT ...."

If we take a business view of our professional activities, we are further in a position to make good decisions about priorities. When we are faced with multiple to-dos and competing demands, it is helpful to step back and ask which ones rank higher when it comes to delivering business value.

Such a view does not preclude compassion and the inclination to go the extra mile. It simply provides a tool for justifying our determination of resource allocation: Will taking care of A be a better investment for the organization than dealing with B?

Business case thinking, attention to return on investment (of effort as well as money), concern about value for clients, and the willingness to let go of "theoretical ideals" in the face of reality ... those are the hallmarks of successful business entrepreneurs. We owe our constituents nothing less.

4.5 What are the "non-obvious" jobs called?

On those occasions when I speak about information professional careers, I describe organizational environments in which information management skills make a difference and attempt to paint a picture of careers for information professionals outside the core settings of libraries, information centres, archives, and records and IT departments. Not surprisingly, a common question is "what does a job posting look like for those nonstandard positions?"

Holders of fresh credentials in information management are relevant applicants for positions with titles containing such terms as "analyst", "officer", "examiner", or "specialist" in the public sector. In the private sector, position titles could in addition include such words as "associate" or "representative" to describe, for example, roles in customer service, client and public relations, marketing, and any organizational unit depending heavily on research, environmental scanning, and analysis of data.

The key for job seekers is that professional positions in all domains call for considerable skills in information management. The challenge is to craft an application and resume that will grab the attention of the hirers—a task requiring casting information management expertise in the terms related to the operations and goals of the organization in question.

As you read this chapter, please keep in mind: Pitching your qualifications is all about how the potential employer will be better off with you on the team.

Information professionals as transportation managers? You bet!

In every airport or railway station, I seek opportunities to watch employees who handle all the background activity—fuel pumping, cargo loading, cleaning, and so on—because I am fascinated with the orchestration of processes resulting in passengers being invited to march on board. Yet the work I am able to *see* is just the beginning:

What about the information underpinnings of the spoken or recorded messages we hear once inside the planes and trains? How could I even get to the windows overlooking the gate or track area without the IT infrastructure of the check-in kiosks and their underlying information and data management?

In my next life, I will look into engagement in the field of traffic management. For now, I pay attention to the similarity between most organizations and transportation entities: The revenue or funding any enterprise earns must cover a vast array of functions associated with information, data, records, and knowledge to sustain its overt activities, and it would soon be untoward if those functions were to fail.

That's where information professionals come in. We can trace the information flows, find the blockages or gaps, and recommend strategies for dealing with them; we can spot opportunities for streamlining processes to get the necessary information to the right person at the right point in the chain of business transactions; and we can recommend ways to improve customer experience through analysis of the activity evidence at hand.

But we must *promote* our contributions to managing the business process: Yes indeed, we are relevant on the team designing that new rapid transit system. Certainly, we can advise on the customer service center's knowledge base with a view to minimizing callers' wait time. Most assuredly, we will help interpret past customer behaviour for the purposes of new service planning.

The task of convincing employers to hire information professionals for roles in such areas as operational analysis and capacity planning—just to name a few examples related to transportation—remains for us to tackle.

4.6 Where are the non-mainstream jobs? How do you get one?

Organizations already featuring an information or knowledge management center or already aware they need staff with MLIS qualifications typically advertise on information faculties' job boards when they want to fill a position in records management, research, knowledge management, customer service, or IT. But just in case they do not, information professionals should trawl for job openings the websites of organizations such as:

- Museums and archives collecting, protecting, and making accessible various objects (e.g., maps, photos, archeological artifacts, art and design) through such functions as digitization, indexing, and web curation

- News media, publishers, and organizations in the arts and cultural sector

- Aggregators selling access to business, professional, and scientific literature

- Companies selling content management, enterprise search, and software products and services

- Companies offering records management and digitization services

But many other kinds of organizations need the skills sets offered by information professionals:

- Consumer products companies needing to respond to customer preferences and concerns

- Government agencies needing analysts for research, policy development, program delivery, and myriad other functions

- Nonprofits needing skilled donor relations and PR managers
- Specialized manufacturing and technical services enterprises needing expertise in research and documentation management

Let's look at some postings statements characteristic of those found in business and management categories on job board websites and compare our skills against them. The following examples are typical of postings from organizations <u>unlikely to post on job boards focused on information professionals</u>:

Sample A: Project manager

- Plan and manage multiple projects using best practices, relevant software, and sound judgment
- Partner with project stakeholders throughout all business divisions
- Oversee the work of external consultants
- Advise management on expected business outcomes
- Develop and deliver presentations to management and clients
- Manage stakeholder relations and communications

Though such a description might not strike an information professional as matching his or her qualifications, a closer look reveals otherwise:

- *In order to plan and manage projects, information from a wide range of sources must be acquired, organized, and applied*
- *Partnerships require knowledge of the partners' situations, priorities, and needs*
- *Supervisory responsibilities likewise require insight and understanding*

(Cont'd)

- *Assessing outcomes necessitates the synthesis of diverse streams of data*
- *Preparing presentations, newsletters, briefings, and the like calls for skills in arraying information clearly and effectively*

Sample B: Instructional program coordinator

- Conduct requirements analyses to identify learning needs and recommend appropriate methods of delivery of instructional programs
- Develop teaching materials, coordinate delivery, and set up and manage a credits tracking program
- Support subject matter experts in transferring their knowledge into effective teaching materials
- Convert existing material into web format
- Manage employer outreach programs and marketing collateral

Here, the information professional with an interest in education would find relevant professional challenges calling upon core information skills:

- *Needs analyses must be designed, planned, and executed with knowledge of the target market*
- *Content development and any kind of system design and maintenance are right up our alley*
- *Organizing knowledge into suitable chunks for teaching purposes is similarly something we know how to do*
- *Naturally, any web related tasks call on our technical know-how*
- *As with the needs analyses, relationship management with a target group relies on our ability to collect and interpret data about the group*

Sample C: Process analyst

- Conduct business analyses to support the client services team
- Collaborate with IT Support to determine reasons for client reports of malfunction
- Document and update the Client Support knowledge base
- Perform risk analysis for proposed projects
- Support design teams to help "problem-proof" new products
- Develop and implement a testing program

In such a role, the incumbent deploys a number of information skills:

- *Analyzing a large amount of transactional information from help desk interactions with clients requires the ability to classify, see patterns, and draw conclusions*
- *Applying past client interaction information to new detective work similarly requires the ability to make connections between previous and new situations*
- *Developing guidelines for documenting solutions and for keeping a knowledge database up to date is one of our core skills*
- *Another core skill is applying past experience to the analysis of potential risk*
- *An information professional would instinctively organize the knowledge base so that it can effectively be used to predict potential new risk in the development of new offerings*
- *Designing and documenting the results of testing programs calls on the information professional's ability to structure information logically and meticulously*

Sample D: Manager, social media marketing applications

- Set up and implement a social media monitoring program to ensure up-to-the minute awareness of customer sentiment
- Prepare regular "social media sentiment" reports to alert relevant parties regarding potential exposures or opportunities at the earliest possible time
- Select and implement social media tools for internal collaboration
- Derive new product and services functionality recommendations from customer sentiment and competitor intelligence
- Develop an ongoing social media training program for business teams, including such topics as social media ethics
- Create and implement visualizations to highlight key trends impacting product and service development and the industry overall
- Provide consulting to other business units in matters related to social media tools and trends

This job allows the social media savvy information professional to apply information skills to functions we might have called current awareness and business activity monitoring:

- *Monitoring of social media content requires sophisticated skills in applying the principles of search and results analytics and in adapting commercial tools, as does creating visualizations*
- *Training business professionals in the functions, use, and ethics of social media requires an understanding of the audience's existing knowledge so as to design targeted, brief, and effective learning modules*
- *Acting as an advisor to business groups wishing to take social media into account requires the incumbent to stay on the leading edge of new tools and industry developments*

Sample E: Public policy analyst

- Conduct research and create analytical reports with respect to developments affecting public policy
- Derive forecasts of demographic and economic indicators to assist in policy development
- Acquire and analyze statistics and reports to identify areas in need of attention for public policy development
- Liaise with counterparts in related entities for exchange of information and reports
- Coordinate with the research work of other departments to ensure synergy
- Build and maintain an internal repository of relevant literature, reports, and data and ensure intranet access to it
- Keep staff members up to date with regular briefings on pertinent trends and events
- Act as research advisor

While specific experience in the sector in question (education, health, etc.) would likely be a key asset on the part of the applicant, a confident information professional would recognize the match between requirements and skills:

- *Of the eight requirements, six relate to directly to research and data; the remaining two call for skills in communications and relationship building*
- *Identification of key trends from large amounts of data and information is a major theme in the job*
- *The internal repository is familiar territory when it comes to its design and searchability (what kind of indexing, if any?); the particulars of intranet access may require some finesse in working with IT staff*

Sample F: Manager, donor relations

- Advise the Board of Directors as to industry best practices for donor management and retention
- Establish and manage information tracking and sharing mechanisms for donor identification, acknowledgement, and celebration (including long term value calculations and analysis of special campaigns)
- Work closely with Marketing and Communications to manage donor related data and to maintain consistent messaging regarding charitable priorities (including visual identity through logo management, rewards design, etc.)
- Produce regular donor and potential donor oriented newsletters
- Manage the research program to identify new donors and determine their interests and preferences
- Craft a communications program to showcase donation impact and support long term donor relationships
- Develop, implement, and oversee a comprehensive donor program for the full range of donors (enterprises, foundations, public sector entities, volunteer groups, and individuals) to provide appropriate options for all donor types

It is a safe bet that information professionals' graduate studies did not include lectures on charitable donations management. That said, consider the applicability of their qualifications:

- *Industry best practices? We know how to identify and summarize those!*
- *Track and share? We are the experts.*
- *Manage data? That's us!*
- *Devise communications strategy and produce newsletters? Definitely.*
- *Manage a research program? Who else would do so but we?*
- *Matching donor benefits to donor types? Can do—it's a matter of investigating the literature, interviewing current donors, and communicating with other charity professionals.*

4.7 Won't I need a new resume for such non-traditional jobs?

In short: Yes, of course. It is my hope that the above examples illustrate how fruitful it might be to pursue job postings appearing in places far removed from the information schools' job boards or the library associations' job listings. The next challenge has to do with how we present ourselves in the application. Clearly, in applying to any of the above jobs, it would not do to present the standard "information professional" resume. A translation is required so that the person receiving the application sees familiar and understandable vocabulary. Let me illustrate.

I am well known for advocating a "tagline" and a set of key-skills bullet points at the top of any resume to give the reader an immediate impression of the key qualifications on offer. Statements suitable as taglines and skills points on a standard library oriented resume include:

- Successful outreach librarian
- Experienced cataloguer of specialized collections
- Archivist and historian with significant accomplishments in specialized curation
- Accomplished researcher supporting teams of scientists

Statements suited for the above job postings A-F might involve, as an example, tailored wording to entice the reader to keep reading:

- Accomplished project manager and communicator
- Skilled communicator to targeted audiences
- Expert researcher and information/data analyst
- Track record in target market analysis

- Successful content developer and disseminator
- Demonstrated skill in analyzing customer interaction data
- Proven results in social media analysis and marketing

Those who hesitate to use the "demonstrated" type words might consider the following expressions as models for building their own customized expressions:

- Bringing to bear experience in ... (research, data analysis, data visualization, social media monitoring, etc.)
- Offering extensive qualifications in research and data analysis
- Applying credentials in information science to customer service management
- Bringing professional information skills to the task of internal content management
- Harnessing and visualizing data for strategy development

In the resume itself or in the cover letter, we then build on such "signal" statements by telling the story of how we **did or could do** something the reader will recognize, using the terminology from the job posting:

DID:

- In my work at X, I managed a number of complex projects to ensure clients received ...
- During my internship, I managed the transformation of curriculum materials to digital ...
- I have successfully completed research into the preferences of a target group and applied the findings to ...
- I have advised business teams as to their potential options based on my monitoring ...

COULD DO:

- My skills in researching and analyzing X are directly relevant for Y as [hiring organization] needs [here restate the job description requirement in your own terms, for example, "to ensure knowledge about past donors and donation patterns are applied appropriately in light of current economic realities"] ...

- My work at X gave me skills I can apply to [hiring organization] as it addresses the need for Y ...

- My experience with X is key to my ability to serve [hiring organization] in its effort to ...

- Research and the summation of key trends were among the hallmarks of my offerings at Z ...

- Communication to stakeholders is based on target group analysis, something I performed when ...

4.8 So far so good. What about the cover letter?

I thank my colleagues who have allowed me in perpetuity to use parts of their fictionalized "before" cover letters (in return for my giving them the customized personalized "after" versions) as material for illustration purposes.

We know that cover letters may not be seen by humans as recruiting software engines parse through applications submitted online. Still, we need them to "nail" our offerings succinctly.

Below is a text sample from a typical application cover letter applying for an information analyst role. My comments are in the right hand column:

Thinking strategically about how organizations can leverage information in order to fulfill their business goals is something that I am passionate about.	Thinking is my passion? Rephrase to focus on benefit to employer
My Masters of Information degree with a specialization in information management and user-centered design has allowed me to hone my skills in analyzing and aligning business and information needs.	Addresses skills but not value
While I may not have the desired three to five years experience as a formal information manager, I believe my experience, education, and commitment to continually improving information use, makes me a good fit for the role.	Instead of calling attention to gaps, provide evidence as to what is on offer
Please find attached my resume, which provides more details about my skills, education, and previous employment.	Delete as it adds no useful information
I look forward to speaking with you at your earliest convenience about how my background and expertise might serve the current and future information management needs of your company. Thank you for your time and consideration.	Balance between confidence and courtesy—but too long

Here's how it might be recast to speak directly (and briefly) to the hirer's needs:

I bring to bear information and management skills on X's business goals. In past roles, I have achieved/carried out/ implemented ….	Speak to value offered

(Cont'd)

My Masters of Information degree with a specialization in information management and user-centered design strengthened my skills in analyzing and aligning business and information needs with business teams:	Here is how I offer value from past experience
• **X will benefit from the experience I gained at Y when I researched user needs and then designed and implemented a tracking system for client interactions.**	Give specifics in the language of the hirer
• **During my work in an information management role at Z, I applied my experience and commitment to improving the use of data and information in supporting stakeholders' requirements.**	
I look forward to speaking with you at your earliest convenience about how I will make a positive difference in your team. Thank you for your time and consideration.	Briefly request an interview.

Here is an example of a potential cover letter illustrating how to speak point for point to the requirements listed in a job posting. An applicant for the position in Sample F above might write as shown below (ordering the bullets in order of perceived priority per the posting):

> You are looking for a team member to enhance donor relations and increase the relevance of the donor services unit for the existing and potential donor community. I will directly benefit your team by applying my experience in client facing roles, event planning and customer service, and journalism. Specifically, I offer:
>
> *(Cont'd)*

- **Data management**: In the client services team at X, I designed and implemented a data tracking system to monitor client activity. I built in functionality to alert the team to pattern deviations so that we could react appropriately.

- **Customer service and sales experience**: At Y, I responded to complex client needs and proposed new services based on the nature of the requests received. I consistently up-sold clients upon successfully resolving the initial matter, and clients appreciated my follow-up.

- **Proactive relationship building and marketing**: I launched a thematic event series for Z's marketing department to involve less active clients. By featuring aspects of services they previously did not know about, I increased awareness in a positive environment. More than half of the event attendees increased their purchasing by at least 30% over the next two years.

- **Loyalty development through targeted communications**: As editor of a small specialized magazine, I learned how to address the readers and engage them in discussions of topics they cared about. I set up a reader advisory group to guide me on developing areas of interest and to identify potential stories. A reader satisfaction survey pointed to the magazine's relevant coverage as the key reason for subscribers' loyalty.

I look forward to doing my part to support your dedication to evolving with the donor community and thank you for considering interviewing me.

4.9 But ... what if there are significant gaps between the posting and my qualifications?

The short answer is: "Never mind!" Let me explain: it is pointless to second guess "the hiring organization would not be interested in me because ...." If you feel in your bones that you could do the job, stage a monologue in which you explain to yourself how "I can perform the tasks because I ...." Then, fashion those reasons into statements using, as much as possible, the vocabulary of the posting.

Granted, an automated selection system used by the hiring organization may still reject your application based on the algorithms in place. But nothing stops you from maximizing your chances by matching, item by item, a statement of your experience with the stated requirements. It goes like this:

- The posting asks for an MBA, and you offer: "I developed successful partnerships with an audience of business administration professionals who had high expectations of proactive and very fast service."

- The posting asks for an MSW, and you offer: "I have social work expertise from 15 years of working and volunteering with a community program. I developed an understanding of the needs and challenges related to the providing the service as well as knowledge of the clientele being served."

- The posting asks for a science degree, and you offer: "Working with a user group of environmental science experts, I gained detailed insight into their typical projects and work processes."

Using such matching of experience to requested education is not foolproof, of course. Still, you owe it to yourself to make the effort in spite of falling short, strictly, on a given point of the posting.

4.10 The classic dilemma of work experience

How do you get job experience when you don't have the experience to get a job? How does one establish a unique skillset—early in one's career—to match specific and detailed requirements set out in job postings? The keen right-out-of-school graduate may indeed lack specific experience but does offer—and should (IMHO) position it in applications—a set of capabilities potential employers ought to appreciate. I count among them exposure to current technology, familiarity with social media, skills in "looking into" the latest developments and market offerings, and a flexible attitude with a hefty dose of willingness to go the extra mile.

That said, gaining while still in school or while working in any current job the concrete knowledge described in job postings requires creative strategies. It is a challenge to fit independent learning and research into the existing academic or professional work load—attending local meetups, bartering favors with colleagues in return for exposure to specific tools, and similar investments all require time. Here are some approaches to ponder as early as possible in one's career:

- Mine the job descriptions on online job boards to get a sense what skills and experience are in demand.

- Zero in on functions that appeal to your personal interests.

- Match each set of functions and skills with potential volunteer roles in order to be able to list on the resume actual relevant experience:

  - If you wish to demonstrate web related skills, could a local association or non-profit use your volunteered services to manage its website?

  - If project management appeals to you, could you acquire relevant skills by taking on a volunteer role in developing and staging a conference or in bringing online a special collection of historical material?

  - If client relations or client support functions appear to be a good fit with your professional personality, might you seek out opportunities to "man the phones" in a local charity's campaign?

Look for opportunities to take on a special project in the current job (these illustrations are meant to inspire investigation; some environments, not to mention bosses, are more receptive to intrapreneurship than others are):

- Is there evidence that the customer support call center lacks a reliable "bible" of answers to callers' questions? Could you offer to undertake a pilot project to build such a knowledge base from the material held by the call centre agents?

- Has the intranet become difficult to navigate? Could you offer to develop a new navigation structure?

- Is the marketing collateral dated? Could you offer to re-vamp it?

4.11 Could intermediation become respectable again?

In collegial discussions about trends having affected our careers, disintermediation often gets attention. The doing away with the research intermediary transformed our profession irrevocably and entirely altered the way in which we serve, and communicate about our services to, our clients. It took some time, but in the end we collectively decided "the intermediation train had left the station" and got on with myriad ways of assisting our clients in doing their own research. To no one's surprise, the "everyone for himself" research model generated a lot of dissatisfaction, in turn feeding a busy industry of public search providers and vendors of enterprise search solutions. Users looking for information have a lot of options but often express dismay at the bewildering variety of those options and the impossibility of determining which ones are preferable.

Now, a different term offers the intriguing possibility of the train returning: Curation. Typically associated with archives or museums, the term refers to the act of collecting and arranging for others' viewing a number of objects—a wiki manager curates the content in it or a content manager is the curator of intranet information. If the curator in question happens to be an expert whose judgment can be trusted in terms of what information to collect and arrange—and in some cases with respect to any commentary provided—those making use of the curated collection have a high level of confidence they are spared all the useless clutter and are offered "just the good stuff." When I hear "the best place to get X type information is Y source, right?" I know the inquirer is looking for such confidence.

In a twist on traditional indexing and abstracting services whose goal was and is comprehensive coverage of a defined body of scientific or professional or news sources, some bloggers and organizations focusing on a particular subject matter have established themselves over time as authoritative sources of guidance. In effect, they become "first port of call" because they consistently provide good quality results for users.

In the past, we held the intermediary role when our clients came to us, described the research need at hand, and went about their business knowing we would, in the time agreed, deliver (at least a solid first pass at) useful information. Now, we can occupy a new version of the role when we take it upon ourselves to curate—select and comment on—information for clients with special interests. The key differentiator between old style current awareness ("here is today's harvest of content mentioning topic X") and curation ("here is what I believe warrants your time today regarding topic X and why") is ... yes, judgment and knowledge. Some information professionals have shied away from applying it, believing clients are the ones to judge for themselves; however—in my humble opinion—today's realities deny clients the luxury of reviewing large amounts of information. As business partners with our clients, we owe them the service of curation—intermediation with expertise. Sure, that will open the age old generalist-vs-subject-matter-specialist conversation ... but isn't that a good thing as we keep working to refine our roles and enhance our professional value?

4.12 Oh, I could never take a job in sales!

Many have been the times such a comment was made to me. Guess what? Any job in the information profession *is* in sales! We start by selling our skills to a potential employer and move on to selling the idea to a subject matter expert that spending time with us will pay off in productivity for him or her. We sell to managers the concept that investing in this or that tool will benefit the organization, and we sell to project managers the notion that having an information professional on the team is a wise move. Selling in the traditional sense—of assisting in the completion of a purchase—is no different.

Succeeding after graduate school is heavily dependent on skills in interpersonal relations, networking, negotiation, committee management, communicating in ways that are appropriate for the target audience, and so on (the shorthand expression is "schmoozing skills"). Any kind of client relations function demands that we have well developed sales skills as we are, in fact, selling to the customer the belief that our organization is reliable, capable, and trustworthy.

That said, there are challenges inherent in an actual sales role. A few colleagues who have "gone over to the other side" have contrasted library work with what they felt was a more daunting exposure as vendor representatives. They were right on the money in identifying a key feature of the front line job experience of vendor representatives: Unable to promise any kind of product or service enhancement and unable to provide technical detail explaining, say, a functionality glitch, they are in the hot seat in two ways: They are expected by their employers to portray products and services in a positive light with consummate professionalism; and they are expected to react to any criticism with equally consummate poise. Fortunately, customers tend to be understanding when they feel they are hearing the full story. One thing customers value especially highly is the ability of a vendor representative to make executive decisions—granting a free trial of an online service, for example.

Therefore, let us sell to vendor employers the insight that giving their new representatives as much leeway as possible in the customer relationship—after all, it's a win-win when the (potential) customer is pleased and when the representative experiences the satisfaction of making it happen. If you are looking for work and feel uneasy about a vendor role, let me assure you: Customer facing positions in the information industry are perfect for information professionals. Your value proposition for getting hired is that potential customers react well to dealing with a fellow professional. Your value to the employer over time is the "consultative selling" you are able to execute as you assist customers select the best options, implement them, promote a new product to end users, and so on.

4.13 Where do opportunities—to find work and to hire—come from?

Where do our opportunities—for finding professional employment and for finding the best candidates to hire—come from? Of course we have already laid the base for attracting opportunities. We know that having a professional blog supports our statements of expertise. We have a resume and LinkedIn profile doing us justice. We participate appropriately in discussion groups. We carry a micro-resume (key professional skills shown on the back of a business card) and hand it out liberally so as to increase the number of instances when someone looks at it. Our organizations' websites have a "career" section that entices applicants. But beyond ensuring we are findable, can we further generate opportunities? Yes, we can.

To take the opportunities that fit us, participating in professional events is one must-do activity in maximizing our choices. Conferences provide a concentrated set of circumstances that inherently stack up opportunities to (1) make a positive impression on someone who may hire us or mention us to hirers they know and to (2) find candidates who offer the skills needed for a position. Active job seekers and those currently employed seize the moment when they participate actively in conference sessions, chat up people they meet at social events, and engage exhibitors in conversations. Employers on the lookout for good applicants to hire likewise recognize the opportunity inherent in being at the conference. Sometimes, an opportunity appears out of the blue. But add to the farming method of "plant, water, fertilize" the conference method of "show up, participate, prowl the exhibits." You cannot lose.

Note: A designated seating area where information industry vendors and job seekers may meet for informal discussions could be a good addition to any exhibit hall. Just a thought.

Information management close to home: A crucial component in "Instructions for Relatives" documents

Sad though it is, managing the digital legacies of deceased persons presents a new opportunity for information professionals. It may become more common and routine for individuals to include in their legal instructions specific wishes related to electronic content, but many who intend to "get around to it some day" will not make it in time.

Following the tragic and untimely passing of a colleague, a friend of his reached out to me for suggestions as to "what to do with his manuscripts." Having corresponded with my colleague for some years about those manuscripts (some of which but not all were available in various online publishing portals), I encouraged that somehow they be harvested from multiple locations and made available in one place for the general enjoyment of interested readers in future. In addition, I mentioned the disposition of profiles on social media sites.

The friend embarked upon a project turning out to be far more extensive and time consuming than we could have anticipated. It's a painful topic, but the simple implications with respect to what we need to leave behind are worth pondering:

1. Anyone can download or recreate what is available on public websites. What about the trove of materials in computers, mobile devices, sticks, and free cloud storage locations? For example, could it be that a massive report, book, or other significant item was close to completion, needing only a bit of work on the part of someone familiar with the project for it to be sent on to the intended recipient or be published? Without access to file locations and passwords, executors may be unable to retrieve anything at all.

(Cont'd)

2. Anticipate the need to remove "ghost" websites and blogs. Of course, any paid accounts automatically close when the bills go unpaid at the end of the subscription period, so a deceased's website(s) and blog(s) will eventually disappear; but it may be advisable to actively remove, upon harvesting any wanted content, the presences owned by the deceased. Provide executors with detailed contact information for domain registrars and web hosts and sign an authorization form for use in conjunction with proof of death.

3. Anticipate the need to delete profiles from social media sites. Equip executors and power-of-attorney holders with the instruments required to prove they are indeed authorized to request the disposition of the profiles in question. Document the procedure required by each company (host A requires B documentation, and social media site C requires a copy of D form with a death certificate) in order to save the executors many hours of research. In addition, it is helpful for executors to have guidance with respect to any desires regarding a memorial virtual presence. To the special file folder containing insurance and banking information, we ought to add all the information our executors will need to deal appropriately with our electronic legacy when we're gone, along with explicit instructions for the further disposition of content.

4.14 How about going independent?

As I have been a self employed information professional since 1992, I am often asked about that life. Working free lance is definitely worth considering—even if it does not turn out to go on for as long as it has in my case. Being ready to offer your skills to clients on a project basis is a wise strategy for periods between jobs. In other words, you need not abandon the prospect of future employment; all you are doing until you do find the perfect job is to put your skills to work temporarily for clients needing assistance not warranting a full time permanent hire. Job seekers typically have a business card to hand out for distribution far and wide ("please, would you take a couple and share them with others who might have need of my skills?"); such a business card could state, in addition to the key features of professional qualifications, that you are available for project work.

Certain tax implications need attention, but it is a simple matter to set up as a sole proprietorship (the precise vocabulary for a "one-person business" varies from country to country). So long as the business registration is renewed when required, the business may persist even though you again take employment. Of course, branding and professional visibility take on special significance if you would like it known beyond a word-of-mouth circle that your shop is open for business.

Offering your services to an established consultant is a good way of finding income between jobs; once again we acknowledge the benefit of good networks. We consultants derive great benefit from being able to draw on colleagues and form teams to offer our clients the precise mix of skills required for a given project. In addition, we gain valuable insight from each engagement. As typical projects are a few months in duration, you could look at free lance work as a strong advantage in letting you assemble a variety of experience in a relatively short time and in building a list of individuals in a position to speak well of your work.

Inasmuch as finding contract work is most often a matter of personal referral (we do not work in the sphere of government bid solicitations for road construction), a wide network is helpful. Recent graduates sometimes ask me if it is a disadvantage not to have a good number of work years behind them. My take on that question is that too many factors play a role to say yes or no. A new graduate with in-demand skills has just as much opportunity for contract work as does a seasoned professional.

It is very much a personal matter whether working as an independent is an attractive option. Some may discover they love the flexibility and variety of project work for a series of clients; others may decide their time is better spent on a full time job search. If the independent work style does have appeal, you will want to find out about the association focusing on independent information professionals.

►►► *WHAT DO YOU THINK, LIN AND BRUNO?*

Lin has just graduated from information school. Bruno will graduate in a few months. They are highly motivated to get their careers started.

Bruno: Our curriculum did not allow much time to think about everything you have said here. I'm having a bit of trouble connecting some of the papers I wrote to the kinds of jobs you describe, much less to being an independent.

Lin: No kidding. Aside from a couple of guest lectures where the invited practitioner did speak to non-traditional jobs, it was not a focus how our skills could be deployed across the wide gamut of organizations out there.

Have you seen job postings for positons that intrigued you?

Lin: Yes, and I have a worry. What if I get a job, say, as a stakeholder relations manager for a non-profit ... what if it turns out I'm good at it ... what if that leads to another job in that vein ... would I eventually lose touch with the information profession and find it impossible to get a more mainstream job?

Bruno: I was wondering the same thing. Is it more suitable for information professionals a little further on in their careers to venture outside the fold ... or is it really OK for us to do so right out of school?

(Cont'd)

Glad you asked. First off, you should never lose touch with your roots, so to speak. No matter what kind of job you take, you should be active in the information associations to build and maintain a network of fellow professionals working in all kinds of jobs. That way, you keep the doors open and remain on the radars of people who could one day prove instrumental for your further career. But secondly, you may want to keep in mind that performing well at any job in itself leads to new opportunities. Ex-librarians who moved into policy analyst roles have told me they'd never go back—they are having too much fun in their new careers. But there's even more to consider.

*What if you were to find yourself in positions with the influence to produce positive impact beyond your wildest information school imagination? Would it really matter that you "left your roots" as you call it, if the slightly-off-the-beaten-path career track you go down one day has you running campaigns and managing relationships with prominent people yielding vast sums of money for medical research? How would you feel about being on the team **handing out** charitable money for worthy causes? Would it bother you to be the right hand aide, entrusted with the most confidential materials and meetings, to someone at the helm of a large corporation? Just asking. OK, I may be laying it on a bit thick, but I'm sure you get my drift.*

Lin: Of course, such careers sound … different yet worth considering. I guess there would be new skills to add along the way— just as my skills could be useful in those settings you mention. After all, information management **is** very much at the heart of major charity drives and of the decisions that get made at the mahogany tables in board rooms.

Bruno: So you are saying that right out of the gate, with the ink barely dry on my diploma, I could apply for one of those secretary-to-the-board-of-directors type jobs with huge legal implications if I mess up?

(Cont'd)

You certainly could if you master the art of matching your resume and your cover letter to the aspirations of the hiring organization. Remember, the person writing the job posting may never have heard of an MI degree. Sure, you'd be concerned about making errors—but you would also be wise enough to verify the rules if you were uncertain about anything ... until you got your sea legs.

Lin: Would it be far-fetched if I speculated that in such positions, over time we would in fact be able to clamor for the hiring of some librarians in the organization to ensure we were on the leading edge of demographic and economic trends, industry news, and so on?

Now you are talking! Yes indeed. If you have the appetite for doing business in the broadest sense, then you could ultimately provide career paths for those who are just in kindergarten now. Granted, a career in business or government may pose cultural challenges if you are unfamiliar with the way things are done in large companies and regional and national public sector entities. But I trust you are fast learners with sensitivity to your environment.

Bruno: It never occurred to me to operate in such rarefied environments ... but you have opened my eyes to a whole new set of possibilities.

Lin: Ditto ... I am going to apply for that customer relations job I just saw earlier today!

Remember, if at any time you feel a particular environment is not for you, it is perfectly acceptable—in fact, it is your obligation to yourself and to the employer—to seek out another one more closely aligned with your personal values. Some people are happy in large corporations, others prefer start-up innovator environments, yet others flourish in government settings. It's just a preference.

5

Organizational operations: The information professional's opportunity to add value

In Chapter 4, we looked at nontraditional roles information professionals can fill. Here, we discuss opportunities information professionals may uncover once they are working inside an organization. All enterprises contain information-centric functions, and information professionals have a great deal to offer to those working in such functions. Our task is to identify the opportunities and be ready to demonstrate our relevance should it happen that our current role gets phased out.

The small essays below are intended to illustrate how typical organizational activities present situations we may use as inspiration for proposals to enhance business operations (not to mention our own careers).

Note that the term "knowledge worker" refers to someone with an information- and knowledge-focused job or a subject matter expert whose functions are intellectual in nature.

5.1 Managing knowledge worker information supply is a challenge—Get information professionals on it

In my consulting work—assisting clients determine the optimal strategies for supporting knowledge workers—I often see that an information professional (or three, or more, depending on the size of the organization) could be a significant value add ... within the business teams or close to them. Yet, as the number of roles for information professionals as embedded (or portfolio) researchers and information consultants is modest, it is particularly important for information professionals to have practiced the "scary stuff" of business cases, ROI assessments, and similar analyses so as to sell their skills into new roles. In other words, information professionals face an employment landscape in which they are in effect required to sell potential employers on the desirability of creating new positions where unique information skills will contribute to organizational goals. Established information center managers are similarly required to demonstrate the value and ROI of the infrastructure costs they incur for the parent organization; they are in effect becoming agents for hiring and deploying information professionals working directly with subject matter experts. Scary, yes; doable, yes.

What can information professionals do for knowledge workers who are run off their feet, arrive late to meetings because they were held up in a previous one, have their gadgets go off every few minutes, and so on? (No wonder stress levels are off the chart, but that's another conversation.) The challenges for information professionals supporting client populations bombarded with all the flashing and beeping add up: it may be difficult even to get enough of our clients' time to find out what they're up to in their work so we can diagnose needs and design services to match; our messages may be lost in the stream of other messages arriving on their screens and devices; and they may be forced to make do with what they can find quickly because the deadline is 20 minutes away. My modest proposal in that context—built on the evolution of our roles from service providers to business partners—is simple, though likely not so simple to implement. It follows the philosophy that preparation, planning, and contextual knowledge pay off.

It is unrealistic to expect knowledge workers to consult with information professionals day to day, but another type of relationship is worth considering: when information professionals are briefed as to a team's upcoming projects, they are in a position (1) to prepare "backgrounders" to relieve the team members of the effort associated with foundational research, and (2) to monitor for and supply highly targeted notifications of new material of potential interest. There is no point in joining the barrage our clients deal with every day ... our job is to reach them just in time with just the material they need to avoid spending any more of their precious time than they must in that noisy place. Imagine that—they are equipped with the latest in technology and tools, and our aim is to provide our clients a refuge from it all!

5.2 Working with reality: Things have changed ... so can we

A colleague recently commented on the telling implication in being asked "why are you not more distressed at the closure of the organization's library and the placement of the librarians in the research department?" My colleague is known for pragmatism and for a constructive attitude focusing on bringing to bear available resources on the most important challenges; so we naturally discussed the obvious opportunity inherent in any librarian's move into close proximity with employees having knowledge intensive jobs. The closure of a library is never something we greet with joy (being who we are), but it is a reality that decision makers' priorities and perceptions of value will drive their dispositions. The focus of effort—in the situation at hand—must now be on diagnosing and then delivering what will provide most value for the knowledge workers' projects ... library or no library.

Times have changed; let us accept and work within the fact that what in our view may not be ideal is perfectly normal to others. Let us find out as much as we can about the priority activities in the organizations we serve and then devise and promote the optimal mix of services, tools, and content to support those activities. A shift from brokering content and offering traditional research support in assisting knowledge workers navigate internal information holdings and finding their way to the right expert when needed could be a simple example of such a reorientation. Something as relatively straightforward (for us) as curating project-related materials or revamping an intranet interface for greater usability could yield practical value in short order ... but we must get to the point of accepting that yes, we are in *that* business now: anyone with LIS credentials is potentially "in the business" of working with any process, system, or tool an organization uses to support its operations. Our skills are applicable universally to today's evolving business practices ... we just need to acknowledge that fact and turn that acknowledgement to good use. What we may all wish, of course, is that the organizations we serve will each have a strong definition of what knowledge management means to it. If we know clearly how an organization and a team within it sees its knowledge-centric functions, we may in turn articulate how our capabilities could be most productively applied. The process of determining how the clients we serve define for themselves the meaning and applications of knowledge management ... would be a good place for our newly "displaced" librarians to start.

5.3 Precious time: Limiting waste

Over the years, many studies have been conducted to chart the time knowledge workers spend on their various tasks—with a view to diagnosing opportunities for productivity enhancement. Questions include:

- How many professionals report that they spend a lot of time sifting through irrelevant information to find what they need? How many wish they could spend less time handling information volume and more time *using* the information that comes their way?

- Workers typically admit that not being able to find relevant information when needed impedes their productivity, just as they indicate an overall despair at the ever higher "information tsunamis."

- How much time does a knowledge worker spend asking around (who could I be speaking to about X?), attending meetings, and searching for previously created documents?

- How could more time be freed up from hunting for information so as to be devoted to thought, analysis, and creative proposals? It is no wonder knowledge workers are stressed if a majority of their time is spent hunting for information or being in meetings (another form of information work, but one whose productivity varies). Assistance in managing the flow of information—so they can apply their expertise in pursuit of the organization's goals—is required ... but how? Is the solution to be found in technology? Information professionals offer to help establish a REASONABLE flow of RELEVANT information, using their tricks of the trade. With every reduction in the typical knowledge worker's time spent in unproductive information seeking, they contribute value.

Information professionals may benefit their careers by paying attention to such questions and similar ones and then deriving strategic approaches to offer to their employers.

5.4 But there's more. What about all the information NOT present?

I recall several fascinating (read scary) anecdotes how manufacturing companies had to invest vast quantities of man hours—and suffer the resulting customer perception damage—in reproducing or repackaging product ... not because of external calamity, but merely because a key information item was left out of instructions or because an outdated manual was referred to in the absence of awareness a newer one was available. Yes, documentation and procedure manuals are a challenge: difficult to prepare, never mind keep up to date (e.g., because on-the-floor changes in procedure or customer input may not have a vehicle for being communicated to the documentalists reliably), they are sometimes just as difficult for employees to consult conveniently. The impact may be "limited" to needless expense in extra work, delayed shipments, and the like ... but consider that in some cases, public and personal safety could be involved as well.

In the anecdotes, significant losses ensued from something as simple as the lack of a business process documentalist and/or the necessary rigor in (1) keeping process manuals accurate and up to date and (2) making it easy and unavoidable for employees to consult them.

My experience tells me such a scenario is sadly common—in private and public sectors alike. The question, as always, is: How can we promote the understanding and the organizational culture that investment in good information practice and culture is worth it ... if not now, then at some point in the future?

5.5 Can our potential clients even hear us?

We live in an "attention economy" and in a "self-service culture." Bombarded by inputs all day long, our potential clients (be they employers or stakeholders who could benefit from our services) may never discover the value of what we can offer them; and—worse—what they can't imagine, they can't ask for. There is a perfect match between "what they need" and "what we can do"—but the perceptual gap is huge.

Hence our enduring challenge is to describe our services in ways our clients find meaningful. Our words must resonate with employers or members of a community (what's in it for us?). To that end, we must know everything we can about their needs and pain points—so that we can speak to them directly and with relevance, in language they understand. Some say it's a learning curve to drop the professional jargon—I say it's a matter of keeping our work particulars to ourselves. No one cares that (or how) we do content management—but our clients do care about the outcomes: "Save time by ... Reduce risk by ... Get homework help for your children by ... [etc. etc.]."

We must fundamentally examine our activities and let go of ones no longer serving the priority needs of our target audiences. It does not matter how expertly we do X ... if X is not high on the list of our clients' needs! Our highest goal is "knowing and reaching the customers—on their terms." Nothing new here ... it's just that it's a harder goal to reach nowadays when our voices are but a few among the thousands our clients hear every day in their electronic din.

5.6 The cost of thinking "everyone knows"

"I'll see you for coffee at 3 o'clock in Timmie's!" Now, Canada sports among its coffee house chains *Tim Hortons* and *Timothy's World Coffee* ... so you already guessed I waited in the one, she in the other. We could afford to laugh about how easily small ambiguities do in fact lead to tangible consequences (for librarians, no less!). In corporate settings, this very phenomenon of "assumed information" is no cause for laughter. It presents considerable risk and waste of time:

- Filings after February last year were coded in a different way so we split the database rather than recode ... everybody knows. Except the latest-to-arrive team member who for a time could assume there isn't any data prior to March last year!

- Everyone knows "the way we distinguish between emails and memos" because of the records management system implications. Ah, no, the summer intern can't—if there is not an easily found and clearly labeled document setting out the criteria and the treatment rules.

- Two departments have historically had different vocabularies for some similar activities they track. Over time, staff compensate for such differences by memory ... but as time goes on, it becomes clear we miss relevant documents in each department because of the differences in terminology.

You could add your own examples how "assumed knowledge" is not "universal knowledge"—and how as a consequence investigation is needed and time gets wasted, for example, tracking down "why the items from the subcommittee were not included in the list" (because A thought B knew to retrieve them from C database as they were not included in D repository owing to the changeover to a new corporate documentation system).

It is an information professional's contribution to any organization that he or she discovers, and remedies, such "assumed knowledge" risks. Signage, links, lists, intranet design, database structures, taxonomies, and other coding schemes ... whatever it takes, information professionals are ready to protect against the corporate cost of "oh, you didn't know ...?".

5.7 The incredible value of contextual knowledge

Someone unfamiliar with winter weather in Copenhagen may check the data and understandably conclude that with Fahrenheit temperatures in the 40s and occasional showers, a light coat and umbrella will do for a visit. Without the extra knowledge from someone who has spent time there, discomfort could result: *Ah, that coat would be insufficient—you need something to protect against the bone-chilling dampness, the unrelenting whipping wind, and the miserable sideways rain. Don't count on your visit to include the few gust-free and dry days Copenhagen gets in January!*

We could not expect weather data providers to capture such experiential recommendations systematically.

Vacation packing mistakes are quickly remedied through a visit to a store ... but for organizations working to harness intellectual capital, solutions to challenges involving "clothing up the naked data" are more elusive.

Difficult to capture because it is awkward if not impossible to classify and codify for future access in practical ways, extra or contextual knowledge can nevertheless be worth a fortune in saved time and avoided trouble if it surfaces at the right time. Just think how often you may have heard statements similar to:

- "Where I worked previously, we used that product and found ..."

- "Several speakers at the conference I attended last month called to attention how there's more to it than what you read in the literature about ..."

- "I hear so many good things about this small company from colleagues in other firms, perhaps we should look into ..."

- "Didn't this proposal come up a while back? If I remember correctly, there was a situation where ..."

- "If you search the archive, you should be aware that four years ago ..."

- "The trick is to use the *Notes* field to hold the ticket numbers, that's how we track how many ..."

- "Maybe not the place to hold a meeting that time of year because ..."

- "Peter had a workaround for that glitch ..."

Then think of the expense (time and money) and risk (reputation and customer loyalty) inherent in employees fending for themselves, discovering only after months of experimentation that "Peter had a workaround for that glitch."

5.8 But the locals know!

On a road trip, it struck me how often the local maps' road number designations did not correlate with physical road signs. Chalking it up to budgetary constraints hindering the placing of signs, I pondered the phenomenon I call "but the locals know!". That phenomenon may cost enterprises dearly.

The map shows we need to get north onto route 37, transferring in the town of Elmin. We get to Elmin's major lighted intersection—but no route signs are there. Ah—a police car happens by and we roll down windows to hear that "route 37, that would be Elmin Shore Road, back 2 blocks to your left." We make the left turn, and 300 feet down, indeed a sign says "ROUTE 37."

Later that day, we come to an intersection expecting road number signs. None to be seen—but, by recognizing their shape, I espied the back of such signs kitty corner. Go straight and make a U turn in order to see the road number signs. We believe the locals know perfectly the numbers and names of the roads ... but they are not sharing their knowledge with nonlocals through placing signs in a consistent manner.

Translating road sign experience to organizational work raises many questions. As an example: Are there clear "road signs" for new employees coming to work in the organization ... or would the recent hires need to rely on asking around to glean local knowledge? Relying on local lore carries a cost—up front or as it happens, for the newcomer or for the organization. What is the greater cost—making up the "signs" (providing adequate documentation) or dealing with the questions, year in and year out? Moreover, what is the cost in terms of the risk inherent in new staff members making errors or poor judgments because of the lack of accurate or updated documentation for policies or work processes?

5.9 Contingency planning: Think through the priorities if things change suddenly

Having dealt with the broken-ankle immediate "next 20 feet of my life" challenges, I have had the opportunity to ponder the matter of coping with and adjusting to changed circumstances longer term. As I learned how to plan for daily activities and navigate my home (on sports knee pads, the crutches were just too risky), I honed my planning and prioritizing approach: What is the minimum number of knee-steps to get the documents I need from my desk to where my foot is elevated? How about postponing that dental appointment? What items could I assemble on a tray so that I need not leave the chair to get them? Guess what, my friend, that cake I promised to bake ... won't happen!

Information professionals are often faced with the need for such planning. We face secondments, IT revamps, and many other types of new work circumstances—are we ready? How well equipped are we in our jobs to continuing our services in unusual circumstances? What would we do if X, Y, or Z circumstance suddenly changed? What tasks MUST be done and what tasks CAN WAIT TEMPORARILY? What temporary measures can we put in place without risking them becoming permanent? How are we planning to deal with the backlogs accumulating from the temporary situation? Let us hope not to encounter much in the way of unanticipated sudden challenge ... but let's be prepared!

5.10 "There's such a thing?" Nurturing information imagination

A licensed optician arrived for the second time at my doorstep—this time with a finished pair of eyeglasses ready for the final adjustments. The frames were examined the previous week at my dinner table from a selection she had assembled based on a phone conversation and my website photo; the final choice rested on her ability to use examples of my business wardrobe to demonstrate the suitability of certain frame colors.

In accomplishing the transaction effortlessly at home, and in getting frames I would have passed over had I been on my own in the store, I am the beneficiary of information a colleague offered me as I casually mentioned the wear and tear in my current glasses. "There is such a thing as an optician who makes house calls?" was my surprised reaction. Had I thought such practitioners existed, I could easily have looked for one. Not in my imagination, no search.

In the world of information and communication services, such a dynamic is common: if it is not conjured up in thought, it cannot be requested. Knowledge workers are not in a position to look, or ask information professionals to look on their behalf, for materials, tools, and services not even in their dreams. Nor can knowledge workers be expected to imagine and hence inquire about the full sweep of implications arising from our innovative uses and combinations of existing or emerging web services.

Information and communication professionals—taking their own wizardry for granted—may be underestimating that "there's-such-a-thing?" factor. On the other hand, it is a concern for some that we might overdo the "did you know" outreach; but upon reflection, I believe it is better to verify that our knowledge worker clients know of the opportunities we enable than to make the assumption they know.

We cannot insert visions in the minds of knowledge workers. We *can* work on building relationships to help them experience how airing concerns, ideas, and plans with us usually results in the discovery of some new advantage they had not imagined.

5.11 As technology evolves ... How do we (want to) protect memory?

In my youth, I was a prolific letter writer detailing to family and friends the ins and outs of my studies and work. It was amazing to see the cache of letters my father had collected when I went through his papers upon his passing—every letter from me since the late 60s up until about 1987 was there, constituting "the story as told." What happened in 1987? Telephone rates from North America to Europe dropped. When it became possible to have leisurely chats because the per-minute cost fell into a manageable range, there was no further reason to sit at the typewriter. It never occurred to me to consider any kind of legacy or history aspect, but I have told friends tongue in cheek how "historians will be at a loss" as to the details of my work after 1987 ... until the web search tools pick up a different trail, of course.

Organizations dating from before the web may have a similar experience as they used aging media until the web era. If some evidence of current work in an enterprise is largely contained in, say, documents captured in repositories and featured on its intranet and public website, there are well-known methods to keep them. Beyond legal requirements, what do we want to remember—and what do we want the world to be able to discover about our past? How can we feature the value of what we have kept? How can we trace the evolution of our presence? How can we ensure our legacy materials are there to support future research? How could technology developments affect future access by researchers to our collection?

Information professionals will have plenty of opportunity to help their organizations address such questions.

"Constructive bragging"—A fine art deserving more attention

When information professionals perform "miracles" for their clients, they sometimes modestly refrain from touting the accomplishment. That's a pity—for the organization in question, for the information professional in question, and for the profession overall. Good news stories—how the investment in the expertise and content in the information center or library helped the organization move toward its goals or address its challenges—deserve to become well known, and it is our job to make that happen. But fear not—we can raise awareness without any "cringe factor." I know of one information-centric team whose bulletin is eagerly read by constituents because it regularly brings stories about how a specific situation was addressed by the staff or by the tools made available. The "you can, too" value is high, and the factual nature of the stories secures credibility. So let's not be modest and think "well, it's all in day's work" ... instead let's think "how can we tell others about this success in such a way as to add to the overall awareness of what is available from that mysteriously named information professional?". Go ahead, brag away.

5.12 Oh—Just one more thing (thank you, detective Columbo): Priorities matter!

Professional pride is a powerful driver of on-the-job behavior, appropriately so. That said, I find it's often helpful to "step back from the brink of perfection" and ask: Are we here to run the most perfectly managed information center in the world, for example, cataloguing every item to the most stringent standards ... or to help the clients get their jobs done? The answer is obvious.

As always, it's not about doing things right (the way we were taught back at library school) ... it's about doing the right things. And the "right things" ... are the activities that will make a positive difference to our stakeholders. The choice is one we need to make—and sell—every day.

►►► WHAT DO YOU THINK, FRANK AND PAOLA?

Frank has worked for many years as a business process analyst. Paola is the manager of a small client support unit in the same company. Having already moved on from "the fold," they are always on the lookout for opportunities to add value to the organization.

Frank: I have come across so many of the situations you describe in my years here at the company. I could regale you with so many anecdotes how opportunities were missed or information got lost—not because anyone failed in his or her job, but simply because the mechanisms were not in place to ensure corporate memory did get protected and the right people found each other.

Paola: Same story here. I'm often in a position to report to IT or Quality Assurance that a pattern of complaints or billing inquiries has developed in the customer calls my team gets—and then it turns out other departments have in different ways heard of those problems. There seems to be a need for a more coordinated approach to responding to, and of course benefiting from, customer input.

You are typical of many professionals who are alert to activity patterns and who think about the business implications. You remind me of someone who is extremely proactive about delivering insights and analysis the business teams never thought

(Cont'd)

---

to request. He thinks ahead how every service or product can be made to support the business teams even better, and he pushes his staff to think that same way. For him, it's all about helping the business teams be productive and achieve goals ... and funnily enough, he is not terribly worried about his employment security and that of his staff. He has a great deal of support widely in the organization from people who know very well that he is instrumental in their success.

Paola: Funny you should mention that. Earlier in my career, when I was a reference librarian, I was very focused on the research expertise I could offer. It took me a while before I realized the business teams don't care about my credentials or expertise—they care about how they benefit. So I taught myself to begin every sentence with "your team will gain ..." and similar statements focused on "what's in it for them." It is so much more powerful to say "the backgrounders your team will receive for each new project will enable you to get a head start" than to say "we can give you expertly researched information."

Frank: As I'm working with the various business teams, it strikes me how beneficial it would be if our company had a special unit whose sole purpose was to detect and address opportunities to assist the business units work effectively without having to reinvent wheels or discover information when it's too late.

Paola: Yes, a kind of information and knowledge management squad!

Information and knowledge management is challenging in that it's unlike the kinds of record keeping long entrenched in many departments of regulated entities. In supporting efficiencies where the long arm of the law does not impose rigor, we are challenged because we don't have a legal or regulatory stick with which to enforce systems or processes. We are in essence—in the absence of that figurative squad you mentioned Paola—left with subtler influencing tools in addressing the challenges arising from employees not knowing what they can ask for, business teams not having comprehensive document repositories, and so on.

(Cont'd)

Paola: I think you are referring to the fact that information professionals need to schmooze their way into working with the business teams?

Frank: That's what I believe. I have been successful in building relationships allowing me to put in informal proposals for collegial sharing tools and memory databases, for example. My ace was that I had credibility knowing the business of the teams.

You are getting to something important here—credibility. When we come from the outside, it's tricky to be making recommendations to business teams. The way I'd suggest going about introducing new tools or services involves the "chopped liver" angle. What you do is build rapport with key people in a team; then you ask if they'd be willing to act as a pilot test group for an information initiative. You then use the pilot group's input to perfect your service, tool, or initiative—making sure to publish far and wide the names of those who helped. It is beneficial to spread the word about who have worked with us because it lends legitimacy all around. We hope our helpers will speak well of our services whenever colleagues ask "What was that new thing I saw your name attached to on the intranet?"

Then, we use all the input to the hilt. We say "according to the X group's insightful suggestions, we made some adjustments we think you will like" and similarly indicate that we are merely acting on business teams' requests.

Frank: I get it—it's not about us, it's about the business teams. Everything we propose has to fit within their framework and aspirations.

Paola: That is a message I carry when I speak to the students at the local information faculty. I tell them it does not matter, sadly, how well information professionals perform in or manage a corporate information center if they are not closely aligned with the business teams.

Now you are echoing my "nobody buys research" message. We can't sell our craft in isolation, but many will value that our

(Cont'd)

research puts them in a position to reach their goals. No one wants a document repository for its own sake, but many will want the ability to avoid errors, embarrassment, or needless work. We need to speak about our work in terms of the outcome it produces for stakeholders.

Paola and Frank: How true. We learned early on that the days of sitting behind a desk, dishing out information, are so over!

6

Knowledge culture: A key determinant of career opportunities for information professionals

The overall culture of an organization shapes the behaviors of its employees. Its knowledge culture—the beliefs and practices surrounding the treatment of information and knowledge—determines how receptive decision makers are to contributions from information professionals regarding possibilities for improvements. In this chapter, we look at ways in which information professionals may assist their organizations deal with internal information challenges.

6.1 Introduction: Do the right people find out?

The makers of popular TV shows *Undercover Boss* and *Undercover Boss Canada* may not have set out deliberately to create a series based on knowledge and information management—but that is what they succeeded in doing. The show points to the opportunity for information professionals to go "overtcover" to experience the knowledge implications of day-to-day business operations ("show me how you do what you do") and then diagnose all kinds of opportunities for enhancing the flow and depth of knowledge and insight.

The series' premise is a disguised CEO coming to retail/service/operations locations of his or her company as a trainee and being shown the ropes by the manager and other employees in the shop. Conversations cover the details of the job as well as the life situations of the staff. The "trainee" steps off site to tell the camera about the discoveries made, making comments along the lines of "I never realized how our retail sales system caused so much difficulty"; "it's about time we had a method for knowing when equipment needs to be replaced"; "customers love Maria's positive attitude—little could anyone know Maria's challenge caring for her mom." In the course of being instructed in the details of the job, significant business, market, and operational information comes to the attention of the CEO through employee stories in the vein of "it would be nice if we knew in advance what the new lines were so that we could plan the displays and practice our sales pitches"; "it's a strain to carry the buckets up and down the stairs"; "at lunch time, there's a bottleneck at the cash register"; "the merchandise is not suitable for the local demographic, but head office seems to believe every store must have the exact same selection"; "Sally upsells customers by partnering with other stores in the mall." Having been at several locations, the CEO—without disguise—is next seen meeting the featured employees to brief them on initiatives arising from the information they provided.

For an information professional, it is so very satisfying to hear a CEO making statements signaling a path to better business practice: "You obviously have a knack for customer service, so we'd like you to come to head office for a month to help us design our new training program"; "we'll take a look at the merchandise distribution process";

"we'll overhaul the retail point-of-sale software according to your excellent suggestions"; "we'll look at your concept of a frequent-luncher service to reward our loyal customers and cut down on the wait"; "we will install a faucet and drain so that you no longer need to carry buckets." *Undercover Boss* illustrates the corporate cost of executive isolation and showcases the opportunities inherent in good knowledge management. When knowledge of what the front line staff experience and observe day to day is shipped up the line and then attended to by the right people, management benefits from the opportunity to take appropriate action.

In many ways, information professionals are able to identify, and then alert the right people to, circumstances in need of attention. The credibility we discussed in the previous chapter is what makes it possible to do so.

6.2 How much are our services valued at the top?

We information professionals eat, sleep, and breathe "good information practices," but it is not a safe assumption that our conviction of their value is shared by others—for starters, by senior management. Let's be sure to find out just what those in charge of allocating the information center budget think they are getting for their investment! It may be disappointing to discover, for example, that there is low awareness of our contribution to the organization—but such a discovery is the first step toward bridging the perception gap. Once we know how "the corner office" regards the investments in content and staff, we are in a better position to focus our efforts where they will deliver the greatest impact.

Our innate tendency may well be to render service equally to all who ask for it, but doing so could be risky. It is a fact that some people in an organization have more influence on budgets and policies than others do, and it is a fact that some teams are more closely associated with the strategic direction of the enterprise than other teams are. As a consequence, services we deliver to key personnel and strategically crucial teams are likely to have a greater impact, overall, than any of the services we otherwise deliver. Given that our resources and time are not infinite, it behooves us to focus on those areas where our efforts and knowledge will yield the greatest positive results for the organizations we serve. Such a focus does not constitute discrimination; it merely reflects ordinary business practice.

Being the dedicated professionals we are, we are likely to devise means by which every employee in an organization may avail of content and tools we array for them. Then, we turn our attention to supporting the people on whose work the success of the organization truly depends.

6.3 The challenge of proving value: We can count them ... but do they count?

Peter Drucker and others have pointed to the conundrum that "not everything we measure is important, and what is important may be impossible to measure." The topic of "Information Services Return on Investment (ROI)" figures regularly in my professional activities. Here are some key aspects of the challenge associated with demonstrating the return on investment from information centers, libraries, intranets, collaboration tools, and the like:

- The professional literature on ROI from libraries and information centers features quite a few titles sounding promising ... some with publication dates in the 1970s. We have been working on the matter for a long time.

- As examples, perceptions of value derived from research into renewable energy tend to be positive, and few would question the value of diagnostic imaging technology. Such carte blanche acceptance of associated investments is more elusive when it comes to the work of information centers and libraries.

- The fact that many of the costs of information centers are "sunk"—that is, we must pay for library systems and content licenses before the first customer arrives and regardless whether 100 or 1000 employees make use of our content and research service offerings—bedevils us. Cost cannot be scaled with consumption (and to make matters even more complicated, consumption may not be seen as translating into value!).

- Metrics of activity—searches, article downloads, page views, turnstile counts, circulation, reference questions, and so on—are a staple of operational reporting, yet the valid question is raised: What do the numbers mean? Does a count of 5000 views suggest users are confused or indicate users are getting appropriate information in appropriate volume? It is no surprise that executives express difficulty in translating transactional statistics into an understanding of impact.

- Calculations such as time saved by knowledge workers as a result of our assistance point to ROI, but are at best indicative. Moreover, time savings and other soft benefits such as reduced risk and better-informed decision making may be viewed as nice-to-haves in the context of budgetary scrutiny.

To provide context for impact assessment, we need to show the *difference* our work makes: To what kind of decision/policy/project/deliverable was our assistance applied? Was the outcome different from what it might have been without the information or guidance we provided, and if so how?

Although answers to such questions cannot constitute proof of financial ROI, they are essential in demonstrating our contribution to the success of the organizations we serve.

6.4 Aiding corporate memory: An information professional's contribution

Access to information about the thinking and activities of the past involves a challenging conundrum: Post facto access is not enough, and upfront indexing is expensive. Enterprises have made strides as the information industry responded to that challenge with powerful engines to be applied to "everything, no matter where it is kept," but the challenge persists.

For example, information contained in printed or imaged reports may not be detectable by a search engine or catalog search function because the records or metadata for reports aren't sufficiently detailed. The question then is, "could we go back and include in the catalog record the table of contents of a report and abstracts of chapters?" In other words, could we "liberate" the details held in the body of each report? The answer: Certainly we could—if we could afford it. In-depth indexing of information objects to provide intellectually value-added precision and granularity in searching is very expensive because it requires time consuming work by individuals familiar with the subject matters at hand.

Digitization of print materials provides a major boost to information discoverability, but we are all familiar with the avalanche syndrome—what's the use of retrieving a huge list of documents containing a search term any old place in the text? The one paragraph we need right now to solve a particular problem is <u>in there</u> ... but it is beyond our practical reach.

The case for investing in upfront treatment to assure future re-trievability is obvious in concept. Funding the activity is another story. The takeaway for today's information object creators is simple: whenever we consign an object to a repository no matter how informal, let's be mindful to attach metadata containing such vocabulary as might assist future searchers. If the search capability allows for full text search, let's be mindful of using meaningful terminology at appropriate places in the text.

Information professionals add value to their organizations when they propose and support efforts to ensure today's information objects will be findable in future.

6.5 Now why did they do that? It looked like a good idea ... at the time!

The passage of time has a way of veiling what was perfectly clear ... back then. Employee turnover may eliminate the possibility of obtaining personal input as to "why it was decided to do, choose, or prioritize X." In certain circumstances, it is helpful for business teams to understand the reasons for past decisions or strategies so as to see current and future decisions in the proper light. But ... is there a mechanism for documenting the factors in a decision made or an approach chosen? If not, the business team interested in understanding past thinking may be left with nothing other than—that is, if they can be found at all—email exchanges to shed light. A project management policy to capture key drivers for a project may go a long way toward securing this special aspect of corporate memory; all it requires is the assembly of answers to the following sample questions:

1. What situation, event, problem, or opportunity gave rise to the need for a decision? Was it a one-time circumstance

or one likely to recur (so that we may need to consider a policy at some point)?

2. Who "owns" the responsibility for making the decision? Who has relevant input?

3. What is the goal—what are we trying to achieve or avoid? (In part, the question is the inverse of 1.)

4. What data, input, background (etc.) was available and considered at the time of the decision? (This is critical to avoid the risk of hindsight casting a decision in untoward light.)

5. What were the options in addition to doing nothing?

6. What extrinsic factors came into play? (While options A, B, and C all have intrinsic merit, B was chosen because security is the top priority.)

7. Was the decision a consensus, or was it contentious? (No names are needed, but it's helpful later to understand whether there were doubts.)

8. If the decision involved implementation of any kind, who had responsibility for it? What process was in place to ensure it moved forward? What risks were perceived in case implementation fell short of success?

In times of rapid employee turnover, this simple template for capturing "what we were thinking" can be a powerful tool … if it is consistently used. Consulting houses have traditionally used the post-project summary function as a means of capturing lessons learned for the benefit of future work, and after action reviews are familiar in the military as a means of process improvement. Information professionals provide value to their employers when they assist the business teams in contributing to corporate memory capture, even in ways so seemingly simple.

Infovores and selectovores

In keeping clients aware of relevant new developments, a special challenge is tuning the periodic alerts and heads-ups not just to the topic at hand, but also to the recipient's "appetite." When we instigate a flow of current awareness information for clients, it is essential that we gauge their preferred style of consumption ... are they "infovores" who prefer to glance at 50 items to select the 3 they care about because they do not want to lose out on serendipity, or are they "selectovores" who are content with a more limited number of items to look through, relying perhaps on supplementary means of being made aware of key new developments?

It is important to ask up front: "If it's between getting too many hits so you have to scan through many items yourself, or getting too few so you might miss a potentially relevant item ... where do you lean? Do you want a daily notice, or should I batch them weekly?" Time will tell if the client begins to lean differently from the original answer. One helpful value-added service is to categorize the hits in a set of alert results: Of the 15 items on the global market for product category X, these 5 focus on consumer research, these 7 point to trade statistics, and these 3 discuss tariffs. Such groupings walk the line between wholesale forwarding and stepping in to judge on the client's behalf what should be deleted, and they help clients formulate their modification requests ("the trade statistics items are the most useful for me while tariff items can be placed at the end"). As always, appropriate ongoing follow-up with clients is paramount.

6.6 Where are the information sharing stars?

A simple and intriguing performance evaluation approach asks: "Name the top 5 people in your department or across the organization who in your opinion do a great job of sharing information and knowledge for the benefit of others." For managers, the results are gold. These named colleagues are the go-to people who have built a reputation for always having something to offer to help a project, support a specific task, or teach a technique. We information professionals can learn from that phenomenon. "Who in your department is generally considered to be the go-to person, and why? I'm asking in the context of a project to capture expertise and knowledge." Naturally, we want to know what the seekers are looking for—so that we may assess how to support the go-tos. But there's more.

It is possible that by identifying the information sharing stars and the kind of information and knowledge they share, we may lighten their loads and make insight available to a wider circle than just the people who happen to know that "Gretchen is the best person to ask." New employees often report that it took them a very long time to figure out who knows what, and they tell the (costly) tale of the weeks and months it took before they finally did find the answers they were looking for.

Granted, there may be hesitation on the part of the stars. After all, being interrupted constantly may put a damper on productivity, to the detriment of the stars' own careers. We information professionals are uniquely qualified to find the best balance between an undue burden on selected experts on the one hand and wide accessibility of precious knowledge on the other hand.

6.7 Silobreaking: We're in that business, too

Silos are for breaking down—let's make it our business. Much more often than I like to say, I witness employee comments along the lines of "wish we'd known your team had already tackled X—we are struggling with it now." The organizational cost of silos in repeat/duplicate work and missed opportunities is breathtaking.

Can information professionals offer a solution? You bet; expertise and project directories are just the beginning. In any culture where silobreaking is desired and rewarded, we can offer effective strategies for managers to endorse. In cultures not yet aware of the untoward effects of silos, we are in a position to shed light on the organizational and competitive cost of hindrances to effective sharing of discoveries, project plans, and customer input (just to name a few examples) across corporate units.

You might object that information professionals working in corporations may not have the authority to "poke their noses" into organizational reporting practices and inter-unit communications. You would be right. Typically, information professionals in corporations would serve in roles to provide or support research, information, records management, and intranet-related functions, and they may not be in a position to launch examinations of knowledge management practices. That awkward positioning does not, however, prevent them from forming the kinds of relationships with stakeholders that will surface conversations about projects and future plans. (For example, it is legitimate to ask business teams about their future plans so as to ensure the appropriate resources and tools are available to them.) Hearing about a planned initiative on the part of team A and then learning that team B is pondering a similar one enables the information professional to connect the teams. Noticing that similar questions are coming from teams not usually in contact with each other similarly enables the information professional to act as a connector. Being the purveyor of various information tools and intranet content could give the information professional insight into current and future projects as he or she introduces the tools and content.

The essence of silo breaking is listening to subtle signals in communication related to other matters. In that activity, we excel.

6.8 Pattern vigilance: Noticing when something is "off"

Hm, it's odd that the hit count for the new intranet content we just added (with great fanfare) is so low ... wonder why? Hm, the call center agents are sharing how they are overwhelmed by calls from customers complaining about incorrect bills ... wonder what is going on? Hm, requests for industry data on X are coming in fast and furious ... what's up? Hm, it's odd that we are hearing nothing at all from project team Y—there should be a pronounced need for our services ... what could be the reason?

What are the thresholds by which we determine when to say "I've been noticing?" Deviations from current patterns may be legitimate alterations in organizational procedures ... but it never hurts to ask, "Hm, why?"

Information professionals are well equipped to monitor for signals and deviations and then to look into the details so as to determine whether they may be able to supply needed information or offer assistance in other ways. By bringing to the attention of the right people such deviations or oddities as we feel are indicators of opportunity for remedial or enhancing action, information professionals deliver value to their employers.

6.9 Social tools: How may we best apply them?

How can social tools be used to protect and enhance corporate memory and knowledge sharing? The question regarding ownership arises because social tools in many cases have become a de facto repository of significant aspects of corporate memory and a de facto means for knowledge sharing. If no one "owns" such a mechanism, what is the fate of organizational learning, institutional knowledge, and intellectual capital?

As a result of their very nature, social tools play into the innate creativity of knowledge workers and into their tendency to collaborate to rise to any occasion. Thus, the social tools exacerbate the traditional tension between proactively investing in systems and infrastructure to capture corporate memory and facilitate knowledge sharing on the one hand ... and "applying search muscle and heroism" retroactively on the other hand. The number of offerings in the enterprise search market suggests it may be perceived to be too late, in any other than a start-up organization, to take the proactive just-in-case approach: The cost of intellectual content management is too difficult to justify in many environments.

Similarly, the complexity of devising a mechanism whereby knowledge workers may learn of their colleagues' activities at the right time defies upfront solutions and prescribed processes.

So how can we work the social tools—and the inherent human desire to communicate with peers—to the advantage of corporate memory and knowledge sharing? What could managers do to encourage practices and behaviors that will benefit the collective memory and access to knowledge? It is well known how actions that are rewarded get repeated; what rewards will strengthen the likelihood a knowledge worker will take the extra 2 minutes to contribute an insight into the communal heritage—given the typical time pressures? Is it feasible to design and institutionalize a certain set of practices (over and above, let's say, the document/records management systems imposed by the regulatory environment)? How does one foster a culture in which everyone willingly does his or her part to use social tools appropriately to protect knowledge for the future?

Understanding information seeking modes and styles

In discussions with knowledge workers about their information requirements, several distinct modes of looking for something tend to surface. Two common ones are "I need to stay on top of every new publication, conference paper, and blog post dealing with X" or "I want to trace the evolution of current opinion regarding Y." In the first case, the driver is a desire to insure against missing information. The second case represents a look back to benefit from accumulated evidence or accumulated context—something may not have grabbed our attention when it first appeared, but now it does. (The looking-back mode is, of course, illustrated in end-of-year and end-of-decade top-10 lists in which commentators review events or developments to assess what, in retrospect, stands out or appears to have future implications.) Information professionals are well positioned to serve information seekers in those two modes.

In a third mode, it's trickier: "I don't know what I'm looking for, but I'll recognize it when I see it." Here, the information seekers typically wish to mine a wide range of information sources for nuggets triggering ideas or connections, and information professionals rely on their understanding of the clients' projects and concerns, and on "more-like-that" and "forget-that" feedback, to refine their ability to serve up candidate material potentially containing items of interest.

To these seeking modes, we then add individual seeking styles: on one end of a spectrum, some seekers have high tolerance for volume and don't mind scanning through a lot of stuff and following links "just in case something interesting turns up"—in fact appreciate the serendipity—while on the other end, seekers look for information in a systematic way using a set of tried-and-true sources, aiming to isolate quickly a specific answer for the question at hand. Seeking style has

(Cont'd)

---

a further component associated with how much experience a knowledge worker has, how intensely he or she communicates with the peer community, and other aspects influencing confidence that "enough evidence has been collected for the purpose."

Are the various modes and styles associated with subject matter or professions? It could be argued that a preference for precision or comfort with ambiguity might simultaneously inform an individual's choice of academic study and his or her preferred mode and style of information seeking. On the other hand, so many other factors play a role that it may be impossible to connect information seeking behavior to professions beyond some generalizations. (Thesis topic, anyone?) As information professionals, we need a hefty dollop of insight into our clients' individual information seeking modes and styles—and we need to recognize how those modes and styles might change over time as project life cycles evolve, as extrinsic events impinge on policy making, as experts acquire experience, and so on. That's why I use the term "information diagnostic" when describing the activity of getting to know the daily reality in which our current and potential clients work: We diagnose not only what they (think they) need, but also how they prefer to ingest any information we may provide, how much they can absorb at any given time, how wide a net to cast in order to be able to draw their attention to items they would likely never see on their own, etc. Understanding the information seeking modes and styles of the individuals we serve, quite apart from our professional expertise in the relevant information sources, is a factor in building the trust-based professional relationship we wish to have with them.

▶▶▶ *WHAT DO YOU THINK, SARA AND TAMAZ?*

Sara, an information specialist, is setting up a knowledge management team in the headquarters of a restaurant chain. Tamaz is a records manager in a regulatory body.

Sara: All those examples ring true in my experience. In fact, it was watching for years how the organization was missing out on opportunities to benefit from knowledge that finally drove me to build the case for my manager that we needed a dedicated function to formally work with the business groups to optimize their processes. It helped that knowledge management has become an accepted discipline by now.

Tamaz: I'm finding that more and more, the analysts are coming to me for assistance with tools and processes related to internal knowledge going beyond the records we must manage according to legal requirements. They seem to have understood by now that I have something to offer them in coping with information overload and needle-in-haystack situations.

Tell us how you got to where you are today. What factors made you stick your neck out, so to speak?

Tamaz: My story is likely quite common. It began quite casually over lunch at the cafeteria table when one of the analysts said he was having trouble finding a document he was looking for. Several of the others chimed in with me-too comments. I was curious because the document management system supposedly was state of the art and asked if I could have a look. I poked around and discovered the document was hiding because of a simple error made when the document was entered into the system. I suggested a slight modification to the process, and it was a simple matter for IT to make the fix. Then, the analysts began talking about the difficulties they were having keeping track of more elusive information—all the knowledge not embedded within documents. At a conference I had heard about social media tools for internal information sharing, so I looked into it some more and showed them the concept. It was love at first sight for them.

Sara: I recognize the picture. I found out by chance that two different teams were working on developing a loyalty program and put them in touch. They were just as amazed as I was that they could be in the same building and not know another team had an identical brilliant idea. I asked them how long they thought it would have taken for the duplication to be discovered, and they

(Cont'd)

didn't even want to go there. That was a pretty obvious example that the company was lacking formal mechanisms for serendipity, and once I began looking, I found more examples. Can you imagine, a marketing team has precious customer feedback data that could have been incredibly useful for the test kitchen **and** for the procurement people. By the fifth or sixth instance, I decided to put together a formal proposal to create a function with ownership of knowledge management. I knew I needed some evidence, and I had help from the teams in calculating estimates of the cost of duplicated work and the advantages in terms of first-to-market that would have been achieved if we had a way to make sure customer data reached the right people.

Would you say your reputation was helpful in making the teams receptive to your ideas?

Sara: Most definitely. In the years when my role focused on industry information and market statistics and business intelligence, I earned my stripes you might say by being a steady and reliable source of information. I made it my business to find out what the teams were up to, and on many occasions I anticipated what they were going to need and gave it to them before they could even ask. That went over very well. Then one of the team leaders asked me to sit in on their monthly planning meetings, and it wasn't long before other team leaders heard about that and made the same request. That was my big break … I was very conscious of acting like an equal, not like a service provider. I saw myself as a partner in the business, and I made sure to demonstrate that I understood the subject matter the teams were looking at. Without having gradually built up my credibility, I might not have been able to swing the proposal.

Tamaz: For sure credibility is paramount. That, and plain old personal rapport. Some people might find it calculating … I call it strategic. I deliberately sat at different tables in the cafeteria to get to know as many employees as possible, and I boned up on sports and cars and daycare so that I could join the conversations. It's amazing how much easier it is to introduce something new to people when we have already had an in-depth

(Cont'd)

discussion about something they care about. I'm sure my little extras helped too—for example, when an analyst mentioned about his daughter getting engaged and it came up the couple were dreaming about a tropical beach wedding, I researched companies offering that kind of service and made a handy comparison matrix showing offerings and prices and clearly indicating that two of the companies provided superior value for money. People don't forget such a gesture, and it opens the door for more serious conversations later on.

Do you give relationship building advice to your colleagues?

Tamaz: As a matter of fact, I have been asked to give a session at an upcoming association meeting on how to win friends and influence people. I look forward to sharing the stories.

Sara: Sure we do. I believe we must! To this day, we keep hearing from colleagues who find it a challenge to strike up a chat with a stranger. I'm with Tamaz, let's use the cafeteria table or coffee lineup to everyone's advantage.

7

How is my organization doing with information and knowledge? The information professional's checklist

Knowledge management proved a rich opportunity for information professionals to build successful careers—as consultants or as employees managing KM projects or teams in organizations recognizing the value of formal approaches.

In organizations not yet having established formal KM departments or roles, the reasons for not doing so could be many but are likely to include elements of common refrains heard from busy professionals (I paraphrase from numerous interactions over the years):

- There's no time to use the e-room or wiki or read the alerts.

- I have trusted contacts to seek out if I need help.

- I know it sometimes wastes time to be asking around, but it still seems the most effective method for me.

- No KM person can know what my job is, and therefore I don't believe any such person can address my work practices or assist me in any way.

- I'm willing to participate in the discussion on the internal forum, but this week's deliverables take precedence.

In other words, KM may get pushed off today's table because time runs out. That's a pity. In this chapter, we focus on typical organizational functions to illustrate how information professionals may contribute value by pointing out opportunities to achieve benefits such as reduced risk, shorter processing time for resolving customer tickets, earlier detection of competitively valuable signals, and much more.

7.1 The information professional's radar: Adding value through observation

No matter where information professionals may be positioned in an organization, they have opportunities to conduct "mini-audits" of its culture by posing and attempting to answer questions related to information and knowledge related behaviors. Bringing challenges such as hidden costs or financial or reputational risk and opportunities such as enhancements in business processes to the attention of the right people could turn out to be beneficial for the organization. We information professionals are uniquely equipped to look at the activities in an organization through the information and knowledge lens. Subject matter experts focus on their individual projects and deliverables while we focus on the ways data, information, and knowledge are handled. Whether we have been formally asked or not, we are in a position to detect risk and opportunity.

For context, let us acknowledge that "best practices" may be an illusion. Each organization—in fact each department within it, whether by way of geography or function—is a unique mix of purpose, history, resources, individual approaches, and many similar factors. It is impossible to generalize how an enterprise unit *ought* to go about information and knowledge management. What *is* possible is to gauge the level of *awareness* among managers and team members as to the suitability of the practices being followed now or potential new practices to be followed in future.

I believe strongly that information professionals have a tremendous amount to offer their employers when they train a sharp light on operational aspects like the ones illustrated below.

7.2 To start: What signs indicate the "knowledge culture" is healthy or not?

Some overt symptoms provide an immediate indication whether the knowledge culture in an organization is accidental or deliberate. For example, the presence of a Chief Knowledge Officer or similar position with central responsibility for information and knowledge related policies and practices says something about how their importance is perceived. The same would be true if each business line or operational unit has its own knowledge officer. Such procedures as mandatory onboarding courses covering policies and tools related to research and records management tell a story. Job descriptions specifically addressing the required information and knowledge behaviors similarly indicate that the organization's leaders have thought through the benefits of formalizing expectations. It sends a strong signal about the understanding of the impact of good knowledge management when an information or knowledge audit is undertaken from time to time or in connection with specific projects, just as the presence of an entity focusing on knowledge does (the entity could be called a library or an information center or could carry many other labels). Conversely, it could be a giveaway if we hear frequent mentions how long it takes to find the right person to approach for assistance or comments about how difficult it is to use the corporate document management system.

Paying attention to these and many other indicators could open career doors if we turn our observations into proposals and business cases for investments or activities to improve information related processes so as to achieve business goals (better competitive ability, reduced costs, protection against risk, and many other desirable outcomes).

7.3 Is there a library, information, or knowledge center?

Discussions have gone on for as long as we can remember about the best way to name an organizational unit providing information services. The concern that "library" would connote dusty books drove a trend toward variants of "knowledge center"—with the occasional anecdotes that employees did not understand the meaning of the new name and mistook it to refer to, say, an employee training center ("oh you mean the library—why didn't you say so?"). The discussion's longevity underscores the never-ending need to raise awareness among employees about the services a library/information center offers. In choosing an approach to information support for knowledge workers, executives may regard a library or information center as one element in such support; other options exist. These questions are pertinent:

Without a library/information center:

- How are knowledge workers getting the information they need for their work—from within and from outside?

- Could the information gathering task be carried out by others while subject matter experts focus on analysis? (It is possible the topic at hand is of a nature that only domain experts are able to research the relevant sources appropriately.)

- Do employees who came from organizations where they could consult with information experts express a concern over no longer having that ability?

With one:

- Are subject matter experts familiar with the services and content offered, and how and why do they use them?

- Do department managers similarly understand what is on offer and ensure their team members take advantage of the expertise in the library?

- Are regular audits done to align employee needs and library services in light of evolving operational and business realities?

7.4 Is there awareness of options for staying informed?

In just about every project I do, I see evidence of the sentiment that "I want to be informed ... not inundated." People simply do not want information that is not directly actionable, that does not make a difference in current projects, or that does not somehow impart a concrete advantage—right now.

Current awareness is a challenge for many subject matter experts as their working days are chock full.

In knowledge intensive settings, colleagues find it natural to send "did you see this article" type messages. Such well-intentioned sharing may lead to flurries of duplicate exchanges, and over time individual members of the team may hesitate because they do not wish to offend colleagues by suggesting they did NOT see a given item. The end result is that a key item goes unnoticed by the person who could have benefited or that the team is without the opportunity to apply the information in it.

Here are some considerations going into strategies for alleviating that challenge—without ending up being perceived as a nuisance. Information professionals are well placed to examine this space for opportunities:

- When knowledge workers are keenly aware of the need to stay abreast of developments and put effort into maintaining a personal lineup of sources to monitor and/or news "feeds" to receive, it is likely the organizational culture supports such behavior. Conversely, employees may sometimes rely just on conversations with colleagues to stay current.

- Do employees comment how they are uncertain they are fully up to date and express anxiety when they are caught unaware of relevant news?

- Does the culture provide for the time to review new professional news and literature as a necessary part of subject matter experts' ability to stay ahead of the curve?

- Does an embedded librarian or an information center offer customized service to establish, manage, and periodically review a set of current awareness sources?

- Does an embedded librarian or an information center monitor the media and post a daily collection of items of general interest ("what you might want to know about today")?

The implication for information professionals, of course, is that we need to show up at just the right moment with something bang-on relevant to what the client is in the middle of doing. That in turn means, of course, that we need to be on top of what they are doing ... so as to become the "human Googles" they need us to be.

7.5 How well are internal tools supporting employees?

With the rapid evolution of information technology—not to mention senior management's understanding that good information and communication tools are competitive edges—the suite of tools used by knowledge workers is a key component in their ability to deliver quality work. Information professionals have opportunities to raise it with appropriate personnel when they hear employees speak about those tools, and questions like the following should be top of mind:

- Are internal tools—intranets, document repositories, business intelligence feeds, and the like—effective and helpful? Are they intuitive and productive in terms of the time it takes to find needed material?

- Conversely, has content proliferation over time made the tools so cumbersome and confusing that employees abandon them in favor of "asking around"?

- Are there mechanisms for allowing users' suggestions to be implemented for improvement? Are occasional spot checks performed to track the need for revisions?

- Are targeted instructional videos or other help items available for employees to get oriented how to use the tools?

- Do corporate branding policies get in the way of employees' convenience in finding what they need?

7.6 What is the corporate culture for proposals and business cases?

Unlike such must-haves as technology security, competitive security, and compliance with the law, information and knowledge management may not be compelling at budget time. How can information professionals contribute to making the case for investing in tools and personnel for the latter? The following scenarios are illustrative of opportunities for information professionals to identify, propose, and lead projects that will reward the organization in the long run:

- *Silos leading to wheel reinvention*: When it comes to light (possibly through proactive inquiry as to what the business teams are doing) that several teams are engaged in similar projects ... how does such a discovery translate into concrete remedial action?

- *Retirement*: If business teams are repeating earlier work because lessons learned from previous efforts were not identified in a timely manner (before the relevant person or persons retired) ... how does such a discovery translate into a productive strategy?

- *Geography*: When teams are spread over many locations and therefore lack the natural ability to "bump into each other at the cafeteria" ... how can information as to their projects be shared without becoming "noise"?

- *Information object proliferation*: What steps are being taken to deal with the proliferation of documents, presentations, videos, etc. on shared drives and on personal devices?

- *Organic growth gone wild*: If the organization and navigation of a central tool such as an intranet has become less than friendly and intuitive over time due to the constant bolting on of new content, what is the solution?

- *Bibles*: Do customer facing employees have "bibles" of correct information to give out in response to inquiries? Is there a convenient process for adding to such bibles when new discoveries are made?

- *Personal interaction*: Do people in fact prefer to get information from a trusted person rather than from a database? In some organizational cultures, obtaining information from a trusted colleague is preferred over obtaining it from an impersonal source—regardless how authoritative that impersonal source may be. Story telling is a popular topic at conferences, and it is understandable that there is comfort in hearing information from someone we consider to be an expert and someone we know would not go with less than solid information: "If Anna relies on that number, so can I." How might we support information sharing through facilitating personal contact?

It's never too soon to add a librarian

"How should I advise the owner of a start-up company about information support?"

Here's a synopsis of the typical scenario I would pose, having encountered variations on the theme over many years:

Among individuals in a small team working closely together, interaction is immediate and corporate memory is fresh and readily available, just as physical information objects are but a door knock away from anyone else ("sure, I have that report right here").

As the team grows and the volume of accumulated documentation does too, signs begin to appear that information objects—physical or virtual—present a challenge. ("Who has a copy of … ? Where is the market study we purchased last month? Which of these versions of the project report is the official one?") People discover they are spending unjustifiable amounts of time hunting for documents and presentations; the

(Cont'd)

> volume of material held in shared drives or intranet collections proliferates past the point of utility; and "we can't find things" becomes a common complaint.
>
> It gets worse when work is repeated or unnecessary work is done because the memory and evidence of previous relevant efforts can't be found. When management begins looking for a solution, it is often discovered how complex a task it is to address the accumulated backlog of information and at the same time put in place appropriate information related practices for the future.
>
> It is never too soon to plan for the safeguarding and permanent future accessibility of the knowledge invested and developed as the organization grows. And there's a bonus: In addition to their expertise in information and knowledge management, information professionals offer a wide range of skills highly relevant for any entrepreneurial venture.

Information professionals have an unparalleled opportunity to become treasured employees through applying their unique information lens to what they see going on around them and raising the related concerns or new possibilities. As we will discuss in the next chapter, that opportunity is associated with another characteristic of organizational life: Communications.

►►► WHAT DO YOU THINK, OSCAR AND LAURA?

Oscar heads up the customer call center for a retail enterprise. Laura is the senior executive assistant to its CEO.

> **Oscar:** All these examples cement my sense that we are lucky to be working in an organization that values good knowledge management. I always look for ways to turn the "data of the
>
> *(Cont'd)*

day" into a win-win for the company. It's that old "the second time you hear it, it's a coincidence and the seventh time, it's a trend." I'm inspired to continue looking for opportunities to contribute to the success of the company.

Laura: I constantly come across situations where the information professional in me goes "that was a close call—good thing I happened to see that" or "perfect—what a beautiful example of team work." I'm always looking at my work from the point of view of the role I can play in making sure we capture and hold on to information and use it. It is my job to ensure the CEO doesn't miss a thing—I'm talking about market and industry information as well as operational information—so I look at myself as a one-person knowledge management department.

Oscar: I think we are both in a position to do what I call "look, listen, interpret, and convey." I pore over the customer call reports and talk to the agents every day to get a sense of any pattern needing attention. In fact, I'm glad I instituted the once-a-day quick chat routine. The agents know that I will be by their desks every day, and it's amazing what I learn when they share their impressions and thoughts. I humbly think my shop is an industry leader in picking up on early signals from the market for that very reason. I don't believe the agents would necessarily feed me their stories if I hadn't made it so easy for them to do so. In fact, I found out to my horror early on that several of the agents were afraid to bother me! I straightened that out in a hurry—we are in the **business** of paying attention to minute detail and small deviations from typical patterns.

Laura: Too true—that's why I'm proud of my role as a conveyor belt of insight coming from employees to the CEO's office. I have many reasons to be in touch with the VPs and managers, and I strive to find out as much as I can from them about how things are going. That way, I can alert the CEO to areas of opportunity, and I get to put the managers in touch with each other if I discover they are having similar challenges.

Do you have examples how your information background and your special attention to knowledge management made a positive impact where you work?

(Cont'd)

Laura: My favorite example involves a little something I took upon myself. I found out from a couple of IT people I was having coffee with that when an employee leaves, his or her computer is wiped clean. Not only that, they told me, the office or cubicle is cleared of printed materials. My reaction was, "oh, talk about losing documents that might have been very valuable to the successor." Surely, I felt, there would be benefit in having a knowledgeable colleague go through the computer to rescue draft documents and presentations of potential value and to eyeball the office contents before taking them to the shredder. I'm lucky that I have the ear of the person at the top who is able to issue direction with respect to such processes, and my suggested policy was soon made official. I smile knowingly every time I hear how a new employee gush how some binder or file from the previous incumbent was **gold** for getting started in the new job.

Oscar: The agents just casually mentioned how useful it was for them to be able to go into the "product room" to physically look at the particular product the callers were calling about—for example, if the caller was saying something about the bottle cap being difficult to remove, they could see for themselves what kind of cap it was. Actually, the agents have been quite the source of ingenious suggestions for product and packaging improvements—for example, "I see what the caller means. If I were designing that bottle, I'd make the cap a lot wider." But I digress. I began thinking about the product room from the point of view of the time it takes to stock it and keep it in sync with the actual products out there in the stores. Suddenly it occurred to me that the agents have to put the caller on hold to get up and walk to the product room ... eureka! I conceived the idea of a virtual product room—a database of images so the agents could see each product and its packaging from every angle. We get the images from the design people, and it's a snap to zoom the pictures on the screen so we can see the ingredient list, the weight or volume, etc. No more putting the callers on hold ... and what do you know, even that small savings of time from not having to walk away from the desk has resulted in a nice productivity boost from the average call length going down slightly.

(Cont'd)

Your jobs are unusual for information professionals. Do you regret having diverged from the kind of career you might have expected when you were in graduate school?

Laura: Never. My work is challenging and hectic at times, but I take great satisfaction in being able to leverage my information skills. For example, when I started working for the CEO, I noticed how many reports were arriving from the VPs—sales reports, forecasts, research reports, product proposals, you name it. They were all differently formatted, and I somewhat pitied the CEO having to go through all that material. It kept nagging me—there had to be some way to make it easier to take in the key points of each report. Once I understood the nature of what was in each document, I began playing around with a "cover template"—a dashboard type one-pager to highlight key numbers and trends and distill the major points being made. Then I met with each VP to show him or her what I meant, and together we further refined the template. I'm proud to say that every report the CEO gets has such a cover template, and I have been well rewarded for coming up with the idea. In fact, the VPs adopted the practice, so now it's company wide.

Oscar: Are you kidding? This is a dream job I could never have imagined back in school. I do get to apply my information credentials when I analyze the data our system spits out, and I enjoy playing detective when something puzzling comes up. For example, why all of a sudden are we getting a spike in calls about product X from a certain region of the country? Is there something wrong with the product? No—as it turns out, that region was experiencing a particularly hot and humid spell, and customers were wondering if they could still use it even if it had clumped. What with the climate getting ever more extreme, I asked the product people whether it might be an idea to add to the packaging a sentence to the effect that humidity and high temperatures might cause some coagulation in the product with no impact on its use. They're thinking about it.

What would you tell the students in your local information faculty if you were in front of them right now?

Oscar: Folks, there's life beyond the library!

Laura: And a good one, at that!

8

Quality in communications: The information professional's life long career asset

Good information and knowledge management lives and breathes with good communication practices. Yet another opportunity for information professionals lies in the area of contributing to clear, unambiguous, and elegantly presented information.

Naturally, any thinking about communications soon gets around to messaging—that activity we engage in constantly through email and on social media. Reams of literature and courses have been produced to help us avoid pitfalls and become effective using the messaging tools—and anecdotes abound how a small nuance or slipup caused major consternation.

The approach to messaging in an organization (over and above any legal requirements) says a lot about its knowledge culture. The information professional may have a lot to offer colleagues just by assisting them in something so seemingly straightforward as email management. Attention to typical practices may reveal, for example, that email folders are being used as personal information management tools; that rampant CC: copying is overwhelming employees' inboxes; that evolution of thinking and decision making is captured only in long chains of emails and therefore extremely difficult to trace later; and so on. A chat with the IT team—and we are, of course, on very good terms with its members!—may reveal frequent instances of employees pleading to resurrect thousands of archived emails, a sure sign of an information challenge. For information professionals, it would be natural to offer a "tips and tricks" webinar to colleagues to remind everyone of good practices.

Tic-free speaking: Just one of the ways we show professionalism

When we are afforded the opportunity to address an audience—be that audience one person or hundreds—in person, are we ready with a smooth and polished message and the delivery to go with it (think about the highly practiced TED speakers—that will give you the idea)?

When I once needed to record a few sessions for public access, I learned that scripting was my friend. I did not want to sound as if I were reading a text out loud, but I sure did not want any unnecessary "ums" either! Writing out, speaking, and then revising the wording (heavily) for natural delivery was a godsend. The end result (per audience testimony) was that my delivery was smooth, friendly, and eminently easy to understand.

It is expected by audiences large and small that we speak spontaneously, authoritatively, and with passion. That said, why not once and for all get rid of speech tics so as to remove obstacles for listeners in hearing our message? Just as you and I would not want to be recorded or quoted saying "me and Peter are close to finishing the project" (suggesting by such erroneous usage that we might not be on top of the project either!), so too we would not want to obscure our delivery by littering it with such tics as "like," "OK?," "right?," and "you know."

8.1 Would it be better to have a chat?

In many a situation, considerations of careful phrasing and unambiguous expression may be out the door because it is simply a better idea to request a talk. A five-minute conversation could easily move along decisions that might otherwise be delayed by a protracted series of complex memos, just as it might helpfully shed light on background and nuance that would be very difficult to express in writing.

Similarly, a personal conversation could be a good alternative to writing that, if it reached the wrong set of eyes, could cause difficulty (as in "let's not put in writing anything that, in the wrong hands, could be misunderstood").

A special form of courtesy in messaging is the heads-up: "I'm unable to give your message the attention it deserves today but will give it some thought and respond by Thursday" is a helpful gesture toward the writer who might otherwise wonder "was it something I said?" and agonize over how to nudge the nonresponder without becoming a pest.

8.2 Jargon cleanup: Communicating to non-insiders

A spa opened in my neighborhood. I went in to get a price list and was impressed (I could use some of these services) and disappointed (I don't understand what some of the services are). I am not too sure what "St. Tropez" is all about, and within the categories in the brochure, I am lost as to what some of the spa jargon might mean. Not to worry, Google later tells me. But why would any business leave it to me to look up the terms? Would a business not want to appeal to a new clientele unfamiliar with the 'insider' words? The brochure—intended as a sales tool but speaking mostly to the initiated, thus leaving me out in the cold—reminded me how much attention we need to pay to the way we communicate with our own clients. I would tell the spa owner that the brochure is not fully informative for new clients just as I remind everyone in the information profession to be mindful of jargon and constantly ask "will non-insiders know what we mean?"

I attempt to heed such advice when I respond to inquiries as to what I do professionally. It was clear to me long ago that statements like "I offer my clients information audits and strategic planning for their knowledge related functions" would make sense only to a professional peer. Instead, I say variations of "I help my clients to decide how they want to tackle challenges related to information and knowledge."

Whenever we communicate to non-insiders, it would behoove us to do the jargon check (even though, indeed, some audiences, e.g. scientists, are likely to understand our jargon due to their focus on peer reviewed literature). As examples:

Instead of ...	Let's say:
We offer current awareness services	We keep you professionally current by regularly pointing you to relevant news, new publications, upcoming events and conferences, and ongoing blog commentary
We offer reference services	Let us know the topic(s) of interest—we will scour the professional literature and many other sources to create a package of information for you to review
We perform acquisitions	Rather than spending time on buying books yourself, let us know what you are looking for. We'll have the books to you in no time—and as a bonus, we'll record the purchase so others in the organization will be able to discover it's on the premises
We create taxonomies	We ensure corporate documents are tagged appropriately so that they are easily found (if you look for information about mat leave policies, we make sure you'll find also the documents mentioning parental leave)

8.3 "Hidden" knowledge or meaning in language, code, or communication style

Tools for capturing corporate memory are not in short supply, and the marketplace for enterprise search solutions is an active one. But there's a hitch. In the context of information sharing, stored information may not yield full value when it reflects cryptic exchanges between individuals who share a common knowledge environment. Come to think of it ... how often do we all use language that would mystify anyone not on the team? What would a new employee searching a corporate repository for the policy on parental leave extensions make of "Peter, I agree that Case 345 calls for a special assessment, certainly in view of EA-11, as the mat provisions may apply here" (if such a sentence were even found in the search)?

The implications for corporate memory policies are intriguing, and the information professional immediately thinks "here's where a taxonomy and some tagging would do a world of good!" But there's another kind of risk afoot when communication is not explicit: Misperceptions leading to untoward outcomes.

In the small European country from which I hail, residents of a particular region are known for their extreme conservatism in verbal expression—along the lines of "not too shabby, it will do" meaning "superb, truly excellent." Because the style is well understood by fellow citizens in other parts of the country, it is primarily a source of amusement and jokes. It is no joking matter, however, when differences in communication styles cause misunderstanding among business teams or between managers and their groups.

- Here's a scenario: A team has just worked weeks of massive overtime to pull off an "impossible" task. If bonuses aren't in the cards, the exhausted team members look for at least a rousing accolade. None arrives, and they come away feeling disappointed ... and likely uninclined to put in any such effort again. Over in the corner office, the manager meanwhile is still battling his or her challenges and, while appreciative of the team's delivery, is unaware of the extraordinary effort it took to deliver it. Two style matters may be at play: The person delivering the miracle did not go into colorful detail about how hard it was to do the work, and the manager may as yet be unpracticed in the art of, and unfamiliar with the power of, praise and appreciation.

- Here's another: A new team member submits a report on time with considerable pride and waits anxiously for some feedback ... unaware that the recipient's style is to take it for granted that submitted reports will be of high quality. (Others know by now that it's great news if no requests for revisions are received.) It could take some time before the new team member gets over the "what am I, chopped liver?" feeling.

- And a third: A manager brings to the new job a style of communication with the troops that worked well in the previous position but is puzzling to the team members—who don't know quite what to make of it but also don't find a way to bring it up for discussion and clarification. The manager wonders why the teams don't react as expected, and the teams get more perplexed as time goes on.

In such scenarios, we see good intentions but less than ideal outcomes as a result of differences in communication style or assumptions associated with communication. Just as we work on managing information objects and knowledge, so too does the matter of communication style deserve the attention of information professionals. It is always wise to pay attention to the ways in which people in an organization express themselves and to seek "local insight" how to interpret their messages. Such attention is not a large stretch from the skills we apply in the reference interview.

Given the added potential for misinterpretation coming from email and mobile device brevity and the lack of time to read documents properly as opposed to frantically skimming them, it's no surprise many books focus on the matter of interpersonal and enterprise communication.

The takeaway for information and knowledge professionals: Let us not assume that our messages are heard and interpreted the way we intended. Let us not react to messages without considering the background, circumstances, and communication culture. Better to check "I'd like to make sure I fully understand ..." than to carry around a big question mark. It's a good idea to make plain to close colleagues the style of how we communicate ("don't misunderstand, if I get agitated it only means I'm excited about an idea" or "if I fall silent, it only means I'm thinking, not that I am unreceptive")—just as we routinely check from time to time with clients and customers to get a sense how they understood or interpreted our latest messages.

8.4 Do we know the cost of information imprecision?

What is the price to be paid by organizations when information is unclear and confusing and fails to orient people accurately?

Having multiple decades of airport navigation under my belt, I take weather delays and the resulting rerouting in stride. "You need the Service Center, straight ahead" seemed actionable in a European airport ... but straight ahead turned out to feature a Service Center sign pointing directly into a freight elevator. To be on the safe side (as opposed to trusting I could just aim in the general direction), I decided to return to the milling gaggle where another employee helpfully added "near gate 35." A quarter mile later (or so it felt with the carry-on luggage I had wisely decided on, knowing the risk of a missed connection), I reached gate 35 and saw nothing but another 'Service Center' sign pointing back the way I had come. Like a hawk, I circled ... and around two corners stumbled upon a series of counters looking quite service-center-ish. The lines were packed and an employee told me "the wait isn't as long in the service center downstairs." That sounded like an option to consider until another triager instructed "you MUST go downstairs for your transfer." Once down a level, I yet again had to ask a couple of uniformed people in succession in order to find my way (same type of sign pointing into a freight elevator!).

If the signage designers missed the opportunity to hang a few extra signs near gate 35 and downstairs, employees might have compensated by saying, for example, "when you get to gate 35 turn right around the coffee stand and then right again into the shopping area and go just past the jewelry store." It's an untoward scenario when an airport serving millions of people from all over the world supports the cost of the type of information imprecision I experienced: Adding up the employee time needed to deal multiple times with confused travelers goes only part way. What about the airlines having to rebook people who miss connections not because of weather but because they are unable to navigate in time? What about the impact on the travelers themselves?

Could it be that information imprecision, vagueness, or ambiguity might cause the organizational equivalent of missed connections and wasted time from repeatedly redirecting dazed information seekers? Airports may not engage mystery travelers to examine the clarity of their signage and the instructions employees give, but I believe most enterprises could benefit from such an investigation: Just where and how long is the path through the enterprise or intranet maze when someone needs to find something or someone? How useful is the immediately available information? How often must an inquirer return to an informant for clarification? How much cumulative time is needed to arrive at the correct department, person, or data inventory for proper assistance?

I greatly appreciated the employees who helped me in that airport; they were extremely pleasant, courteous, and approachable. But an extra sign here and there—or, say, a map to hand out showing the location of the service center relative to landmarks like gates and coffee stands—would reduce the need for them to deal with quite so many harried passengers. Said another way: I'd venture that a one-time investment in information precision (signs, maps) could pay for itself in no time and then eliminate the year-in, year-out cost of making up for its absence.

8.5 "Do not crush"—information may be accurate yet still ambiguous!

Every day offers lessons in the nuances of communication from the point of view of the recipient's experience. As dealers in information, we need to be sensitive to any potential ambiguity arising from such experience.

Familiar with the implications of some tablets being "enteric coated" and thus not intended for cutting or crushing because the active ingredients need to be released in a specific way in the intestinal tract, I asked a pharmacist regarding the huge antibiotic tablets she had just dispensed, "may I crush or cut them into tiny pieces so that I can swallow them?"

The accompanying literature said "do not crush or chew" but did not provide a reason. She advised that I could go ahead—but it would have been nice if the literature had been unambiguous. It's *if you crush the tablet, the medication won't be effective* or else it's *if you crush the tablet, there will a terrible taste sensation (but the medication will still be effective)*. Either way, I would have been in a position to decide independently what to do with those tablets (for example, ask for the liquid formulation!).

The information in the drug sheet was not incorrect. It just did not take into account the experience a reader might have. When we create messages, our task is to provide the appropriate contextual information for recipients to make a decision. Consider the difference between ...

Please join us Thursday for a quick demonstration of X new resource

... and

It has come to light that complications have arisen in the past due to a misunderstanding about how to use the content on the intranet—please join us Thursday for a quick demonstration of X new resource.

The context in the latter example puts an entirely different light on the invitation, doesn't it?

8.6 Local color: The power of understanding "where the clients are coming from"

The power of shared knowledge in influencing the effectiveness of communication is often illustrated in anecdotes related to "speaking the clients' language" and "understanding the clients' aspirations and concerns." When we information professionals communicate with our target audience to learn what the business teams are planning for next year (so we can support them) or to entice them to make use of our excellent services, we are well advised to put ourselves in their shoes and reflect in our vocabulary the priorities *they* hold (as opposed to extolling our own virtues in library language).

"You are here to lay the foundation for an exciting and rewarding career—and I am here to help you do just that!" could be a message resonating with entry level new hires just as "we're into risk reduction just as you are" might get the attention of business leaders. The more we understand about the challenges experienced by our clients, the better we are in a position to speak directly to those challenges in terms familiar to them—and to leave out the bits about our authoritative resources and unique skills.

I have often used the "47 searchable fields" example to illustrate the point that clients don't care about the features of our tools ... they care about the results they will achieve. That is why users like lawyers and accountants, notorious for overtime work, are more likely to respond to "go home on time" (because our services and tools save you so much time) than to any message about the attributes of the particular information resource we are telling them about.

8.7 Busy decision makers have short attention spans: Communicating quickly and compellingly

To be sure, a business case must be solidly backed up with evidence, indicators, references to published literature, quotes from authorities, and so on. For information professionals advancing and advocating initiatives, it is worth keeping in mind how "it's not about us, it's about the stakeholders." *We do not ask for funding ... the business team leaders do. We are not pushing for change ... the opinion leaders / knowledge workers / sales and client service reps (etc.) are.* By removing ourselves from the equation and advocating from the vantage point of the business benefits desired by recognized influence groups, we may add considerable weight to the proposal at hand. But there's more:

At senior levels, some decisions are made quite quickly—contributing factors could include prior familiarity with the circumstances at hand, previous evidence pointing toward an approach, and the combined voices of stakeholders having chimed in. In the "boardroom moment," there is not enough time to wade through long texts or spreadsheets—instead, punchy visuals summarizing data and illustrating desirable future states can be powerful persuaders. There is a reason data visualization is a hot business area—given the same number of seconds for a person to assimilate information, much more can be understood from visual displays than is possible to assimilate through the written and spoken word. Crystallizing facts and statistics into images to help decision makers understand quickly the key messages could be the factor setting one case apart from others when the votes are cast.

In my book on business cases, I emphasized the value of practicing a business case presentation so that it comes across

with factual heft, research strength, and professional polish
… what I didn't say but wholeheartedly endorse is that our
few minutes in front of the executive committee must also be
vivid and memorable. We are likely one day to be standing
there in the boardroom, having 10 minutes to pitch our proposal and put all our research and previous work into one
concise delivery. Skills in getting and keeping the attention of
a tough audience are paramount!

"Where do I learn such skills?" you may ask. Several colleagues have described the strong boost in confidence they
gained from attending the Toastmasters course. Many av-
enues are available … the key is to be goal oriented about
the need to build skill in engaging an audience. (Of course,
teaming up with people talented in the art of creating visuals
or taking an appropriate continuing education course could
be advantageous.)

Sticky notes

When a publication solicited an article for a "paperless office"
theme issue, I conceived an idea when looking down on the
significant presence of printed matter in my office and wrote a
whimsical piece on the continued utility of paper. After submit-
ting the piece, I kept thinking about the challenge of imparting
information in a format-unpredictable environment.

Just as an example: How would you tell the next owner of
your condo that "owing to the kitchen renovation, access to the
electricals for the dishwasher is from the adjacent bathroom"
without affixing a (plastic encased) note in the circuit breaker
cabinet? Any PDF and paper manual you were to prepare for
new owners—I have created such resources in the past—will get
lost or become inaccurate over time. I have hopes my plastic
encased note will survive for the duration (if it is ever lost, the

(Cont'd)

future owners and their electricians will figure it out, but time will be wasted). Translation to our work: Haven't we all discovered "Oh, we changed the process and now instead we ..." type information that got lost in the mists of email and thus did <u>not</u> get captured in the equivalent of a plastic covered notice?

Unlike a discontinuous residential change, most work places are fluid and continuous in personnel so that practice information is passed on. But it's not a given. I'm sure some knowledge workers have felt as they started their jobs just the way those condo owners felt who had to seek out help to obtain the water shutoff valve tool the previous owners never knew they needed to buy!

The takeaway: How can we help others by alerting them appropriately, via paper or acrylic signs if need be, to information they might not otherwise see?

8.8 Up front or step by step: How do we help readers understand and agree with our thinking?

In situations when we wish to convince readers to adopt a particular view, encourage them to take a specific action, or otherwise get them to come around to our way of thinking, what is the best approach to presenting the information we are conveying? Essentially, the choice is between "state the request up front, then explain the reasons" and "set out the circumstances and the matter to be resolved, explain some options and considerations, then finally state the request or proposed action."

Though the reader may indeed react by thinking "good idea, I can support it," the former option runs the risk that the reader may be put off by the upfront request and, in a frame of mind of opposition and disagreement, fail to fully comprehend the logical thinking presented in the subsequent reasons. In other words, we never get the reader to hear us out.

Though the reader may indeed patiently read through the preambles and explanations, the latter option runs the risk that the reader tires during perusal of the contextual explanations and skips to the end, thus missing out on key information. In other words, we again fail to get the reader to hear us out.

The resolution to the dilemma may in many cases rest within a corporate culture dictating one approach or the other; or we may decide which way to go based on knowledge of the reader's or readers' attitudes and opinions or based on experience. For example, we may take into account how in the past, it worked well to plant a seed of situational information and return later with the proposal or how we were thanked for getting to the point speedily.

As an illustration, imagine how the webmaster (whose baby the website is) might react to each of these two identical messages, differently presented:

▶ **The website is a mess. It needs to be revamped.** Over the last year, there have been many complaints from users that they could not find their way around the site. Clickpaths and abandonment rates support the customer input that there is too much content on each page and that the menus are too long—it seems site visitors get confused and just give up. It is unfortunate for us to lose potential customers, don't you agree?

▶ Over the last year, we have been hearing more and more often from website users saying they could not find their way around the website. It would appear that the very richness of content and menu options could be getting in the way of site visitors' navigation—that is what the clickpaths and abandonment rates are suggesting. While the site's content is impressive, it would be unfortunate if its rapid growth has led to an increased risk of losing potential customers due to their confusion. **Could we meet to discuss a potential strategy for responding to customer input?**

8.9 Vital heads-up—or information clutter?

In a European bank's window envelope, showing through once the contents were removed, appeared the following message: "Should you receive multiple envelopes sent the same day, please be aware that it is cheaper to pay the extra postage than it would be to collect several statements in one envelope. We hope you understand." Hmm ... would some recipients think "that makes sense, glad you told me" and the rest think "why are you telling me this?"

While curious whether the bank's explanation was occasioned by <u>actual</u> or <u>anticipated</u> complaints, I surmise the bank is using the window envelope as a means of communicating with recipients who *may not visit its website*—likely featuring a "click here for more information about multiple mailings on the same day."

The simple example illustrates the quandary we information professionals face from time to time: Will an upfront caveat or announcement show diligence and thus avert subsequent criticism—or will it amount to unnecessary noise for those who are unaffected or unconcerned? Whenever we prepare to communicate broadly, let's ask:

- Do most members of the potential audience need to hear the message? What are the risks if the message were not sent out? How can we label the message so recipients understand whether it applies to them?

- Are there official drivers? (For example, must it be documented that due efforts were undertaken to inform relevant parties of a matter?)

- Is there a way to be brief but provide an option for more information? "New data elements in the corporate directory: For details, ...?"

In today's environment of information overload, it is a necessary courtesy to communicate *in the right amount.*

Every detail counts!

The adage "don't know what you've got till it's gone" came home in spades in the aftermath of an ankle fracture sustained while traveling in Europe. It is amazing how much information we never think about ... until we must. The logistical minutiae of my return to Canada reflected in microcosm how much informational detail we tend to overlook in the activities, projects, and communications we undertake day to day—and reminded me of the need for specific information whenever we plan ahead, no matter what the scope of the tasks at hand.

With many thanks to the airline staffers who got me (with crutches clutched in hand and bag perched on lap) through 4 airports, let me illustrate:

- What is the nature of the surfaces I'm going to be traversing (door thresholds, mats, rugs, marble, gravel, uneven sidewalks, curbs)? Is it even safe to use the crutches?

- How on earth do I get through that giant, and for an inexperienced crutch user dizzyingly fast, revolving door? Who knew there's a button at the side to slow down its speed, as a passerby showed me the second time around?

- When I do get inside the terminal, is there a place to sit while I plot my strategy for "activating" the wheelchair

(Cont'd)

---

service I requested from the airline? The service commences at the check-in counter, not before. If it weren't for my sister running to the counter on my behalf, I would have been reduced to flagging down any uniformed individual passing by my bench inside the terminal doors!

- How far is row 28 from the airplane entry door? It sounds as if it's way down, maybe I ought to ask again for a seat near the front ... oh no, wait, the particular plane model in question has a second door in the tail end!

- Will the other passengers mind if I cling to their arm or back rests as I hopscotch to get to and from my seat (safer than using crutches inside a plane)? Of course not, the white aircast is pretty obvious—but still.

- How far will the wheelchair service take me in the destination airport? All the way out to the taxi stand, thank goodness!

The experience was a striking illustration of the value of *thorough* advance information. Whenever we orient others, design websites, or otherwise carry out our professional functions, it helps to think it through: What else does my client need to be alerted to? What assumptions am I (possibly mistakenly) making about what he or she knows? What isn't likely to be familiar, given the differences, say, between practices in various countries? What small points could potentially cause difficulty if they are not made explicit? Details, details. They matter.

8.10 Clarity check: Do we meet the standards for clear and effective content in messages, website content, and other information objects?

Haven't we all ignored an important email because its poorly worded subject line made it appear to be a routine announcement? Haven't we all been taken aback at what sounded rude but was simply a result of the writer's haste?

In a blog-happy world, casual writing is everywhere. No one seems to mind much if the text is loosely structured or if it contains errors. However, such tolerance carries a risk. "Who cares if the website content wasn't checked by a good editor?" could be a legitimate sentiment in some contexts and could produce reputational damage in others. *Some* readers will in fact conclude "if that's the level of care the organization takes with its client communications, there are untoward implications for the quality of service it will deliver—I'll take my business elsewhere."

In the spirit of "no one's reputation was ever hurt by elegant and concise language," I always encourage attention to the reader's convenience and busy schedule. Let us never put the onus on the reader to deduce what we meant or to wade through wordy passages to get to the point. Let us never run the risk that something written in haste causes unnecessary offense or confusion. Let us always make it clear at the outset what action is needed or why the information below the heading is important.

Throughout our careers, we signal to others the attention we give our responsibilities through the attention we give our writing. Fortunately, the resources at our disposal are vast. (Caution: Text processing software spell checkers are not among the resources to trust. Their suggestions are often wrong.) But what if doubt does not even arise? I have been stunned by the frequency with which highly educated information professionals commit serious usage errors indicating a lack of understanding of underlying grammar, word origins, and the like. Make use of the many grammar help resources available and subject all your written products to a thorough quality control.

The fast pace of work may make for limited opportunities to "smith" our prose as much as we might like—and soaring oratory may be unnecessary in many cases. After all, with our adoption of email and then the ultrabrief message format, we increased our tolerance for formulations that might otherwise be considered a bit rough. However, the common admonition "sleep on that email before you hit send" is a wise one; misunderstanding may be difficult if not impossible to correct after the fact.

What message does poor writing send?

There are reputational implications of poor writing skills on the part of professionals who are routinely required to prepare reports, emails, and other documents. No doubt my information profession colleagues—engaged as they are in many communication tasks—would cringe along with me upon hearing the voiceover in a television commercial for a cleaning product. The commercial declares *"Kids love bath time—but so does bacteria. It hides ..."*. Run that by me one more time? "Bacteria" used with "does" and "hides"... in a huge multinational company's commercial?

For those who have been around the "criterion/criteria" and similar singular/plural choices, the commercial is striking because it raises questions:

1. LACK OF KNOWLEDGE? Did the writers simply not know that "bacteria" is plural? Did no one in the chain of approvals catch the error?

2. DELIBERATE ERROR? Did the writers and the marketing management team believe that incorrect usage would make the commercial more appealing to viewers? Consider that *"so do bacteria. They hide ..."* (1) would not challenge anyone's comprehension and (2) would match better with the plural "kids."

As society evolves along a path of increasing informality in communication, it is understandable that attitudes toward language relax. A grammatical error on a statistical chart may be inconsequential if the numbers are accurate and there is no

(Cont'd)

---

possibility of misunderstanding or ambiguity. Brevity in texting and emails produces shortcuts we all understand. When alerted to an error, some say "oh, I know it's not grammatically correct, but I don't want to be perceived as a stickler!" or "grammatical errors in the text is not a worry at all—at worst, not many readers would notice; at best, it provides some verve to the text!". All in all, we are collectively growing tolerant and unconcerned.

That said, how do information professionals deal with the decreasing sensitivity to language errors? In the spirit of taking the high road, these simple principles apply:

- Grammatical accuracy can never be a liability. Proper usage supports clarity. Clear and correct writing will serve any professional's purposes as it keeps the focus on the message being conveyed and avoids confusing readers or listeners. Deliberate or inadvertent sloppiness is unlikely to produce positive results.

- Consider that decision makers may react to language errors in various ways: Customers likely purchase the product featured in the commercial due to the company's overall product related reputation. However, were I to see a flawed advertisement for a company or product unfamiliar to me, a resume with errors, or a poorly written proposal ... I might hesitate (and that would be a shame if in fact the company, product, person, or proposal had merit).

8.11 Sleeping on it: Ensuring our messages are professionally crafted

With few exceptions, information professionals are called upon to communicate to members of the public (visitors in person or website visitors) or clients (users of content access tools). How are we doing in that task?

These questions are relevant for, and should be applied to, any piece of text we intend to send to others or display publicly:

8.11.1 Does the message "work"?

- Having read the piece, are readers likely to know clearly what action is expected from them?

- If the purpose is anything other than communicating low-risk information, is the tone appropriate and at the right level of intensity?

- Is the level of formality appropriate for the topic and for the relationship between the writer and the readers?

8.11.2 Is the message engaging enough to be read in full?

- Having read the headline or introductory statement, are readers likely to be interested in continuing to read or explore?

- Is the content inspiring and encouraging so that readers are motivated to react in ways we were hoping they would?

- Are we providing convenient and instant means for readers to respond (e.g. "if you would like to know more, click HERE")?

8.11.3 How does the message reflect on the writer (or the writer's team)?

- What impression are readers likely to take away about our expertise?

- Does the message entice readers to get in touch for additional consultation?

- Is the message supportive of and consistent with the content of other communications issued by me or by the team—in other words, does it support trust in our professional skills?

8.11.4 Is the message free of errors or distracting bloopers?

- Are there mistakes with real impact—e.g. "not" where we meant "now"?

- Could plainer words convey the meaning, and did fad expressions sneak in (e.g. "utilize" where "use" would do and "operationalize" where "carry out" would do)?

- Is informal usage cluttering up the reading experience—e.g. "there are many people who believe" or (ouch) "there's many people that believe" where "many believe" would be crisp?

- Is there ambiguity? Sentences starting "This ..." are especially likely to require reformulation: "*A hacking incident uncovered a large loss of data. This caused great concern and much extra work. This was a serious problem.*" Does the first "this" refer to the hacking or the loss of data or the extra work? What does the second "this" refer to? (Avoid beginning a new sentence with "this"—problem solved!)

- Are there outright cringe-inducers like "preventative" and "please let Susan and I know if you need assistance"? [The correct word is "preventive", and the correct expression is "please let Susan and me know."] (See my website, under *Articles*, for a document featuring 98 other examples. It is inexcusable for any information professional to allow language usage errors in his or her written materials ... no matter how commonly they are made by others. Yes, we will all encounter numerous instances of a writer using "myriad of" and "comprised of" ... but those expressions have always been and remain incorrect!)

Once such questions are addressed—we may each have a personal checklist of pitfalls to avoid—wait! Look at the item later, with fresh eyes and a bit of distance. I have been "saved" many a time just by planning ahead for inserting such a delay. Looking at the document one more time enabled me to rephrase for greater accuracy, reorder the sequence of paragraphs for a more logical progression, and add inter-paragraph headlines to help the reader follow along with my thinking. So indeed, in the absence of a different set of eyes … do sleep on it.

8.12 Visuals check: Do we meet the standards for clarity in layout and formatting?

Our memos, cover letters, reports, presentations, marketing collateral (and many other items) are the evidence we leave behind when we exchange materials with colleagues, stakeholders, or clients. That evidence may be all a later viewer has to go on in forming a judgment about the quality of our services and indeed about our overall competence. Fortunately, it is not difficult to develop a unique style to set our materials apart from everyone else's and signal skill through attention to readability and elegance.

Text processing software provides a vast range of tools for arraying text on a page (or a sign) to enhance the ease with which readers understand the content. It behooves information professionals to master those tools and to care for text so as to give it a professional appearance. Just as we would not show up for an important meeting or presentation in gym gear, so too we ensure that our documents do us justice through their professional appearance.

The examples below illustrate simple ways in which we "dress" documents to reflect well on our competence and professionalism.

8.12.1 Simple measures help achieve a professional look

- Unless corporate style prevents it, deliberately select such features as font and font size, header styles, and amount of white space. A modern font (Calibri, Tahoma, Tw Cen MT, Verdana) is a better option than the dated looking Times Roman and Arial.

- Control the distance between paragraphs. When spacing between paragraphs and bullets consists of blank lines as opposed to being automatically imposed by the "paragraph" function, you may tweak their font size so as to slightly increase or decrease the distance between blocks of text, headings and text, and bullets and thus avoid flaws like a single line falling onto the next page.

- Pay attention to opportunities for using graphics conventions (for example, special symbols like ► to signal to readers that "a new topic begins here") to provide structure and give the reader an opportunity to orient quickly as to the content of the document.

- Apply consistent sizes of headings (e.g. new chapter = 16 point bold, subheading = 14 point bold) and color conventions to aid reading (for example, in my reports I use burgundy for chapter headings and dark green for subheadings as they are my "corporate colors"). Decide whether to capitalize words in subheadings and then be consistent.

- Use tables to present or summarize information clearly. Adjust table margins to give the appropriate amount of space around the text in cells (the Microsoft Word default is zero space above and below text in table cells—it looks terrible). Balance the width of columns with the text they need to accommodate to avoid crowded or "bare" columns. Use half-size fonts to compact information without sacrificing readability; for example, if the body text is 11 point, the content of table cells could be 10.5 point. Learn the tricks of merging/splitting cells, forcing a row to begin on a new page, shading cells, and so on.

- Use appropriate justification: "Full" works well for run-on prose, but bullet text and text in table cells should be "left."

- Use color, underline, *italics*, and **bold**—even ***combinations***—for emphasis and effect, but in moderation so as not to make the reader dizzy!

8.12.2 Examples of simple adjustments to enhance clarity and quality of presentation

Compare the ways in which information is presented in the two illustrations below. Would you rather be represented by the first or the second version?

▶ Illustration 1: What message is being sent about you in each of these tables?

Response to requests for participation in an interview

Subject	Faculty		Students	
	# Requests	# Responses	# Requests	# Responses
Science/ Engineering	10	9	12	10
Law/Business	20	17	18	15
Humanities/Arts	7	7	4	3
Total	37	33	34	28

Response to requests for participation in an interview

Subject	Faculty		Students	
	# Requests	# Responses	# Requests	# Responses
Science/Engineering	10	9	12	10
Law/Business	20	17	18	15
Humanities/Arts	7	7	4	3
Total	37	33	34	28

► Illustration 2: How easily will a reader understand each version of the (fictional) summary?

Summary: Proposed Knowledge Audit Process

A three-stage process is proposed for the knowledge audit. In the first phase, the audit team will build an inventory of known repositories (databases, shared drives, etc.); describe each in terms of its nature and size; and indicate who owns and maintains it and who uses it. Any concerns (e.g. it is difficult to use, out of date, etc.) should be noted. In addition, it should be noted how well the existence of each repository is known and what is required for an employee to use it (for example, is assistance required from the owner in searching it and interpreting the results?). In the second phase, interviews and focus groups will probe for employees' experience with the sharing tools they know about and use and solicit input as to desired features. The audit team will probe for the current practices in terms of knowledge sharing (e.g. who is the best person to ask about X?). In particular, the team is looking to identify silos

(Cont'd)

and situations in which expertise remains known only to a select few. In the third phase, the audit team will summarize and interpret the findings and derive initial recommendations for improvements in access to information and access personal expertise. Stakeholders will be given ample opportunity to review and discuss the findings and recommendations with the team before the report is finalized for approval by the executive committee. Once approved, the recommendations will be cast into a plan with estimates of time and resources required for implementation.

Summary: Proposed Knowledge Audit Process	
1. Inventory of Content	
List and describe known repositories	■ With input from IT, prepare inventory of known databases, shared drives, etc. ■ Indicate nature, size, ownership, usage, and other attributes for each ■ Document any concerns associated with each (e.g. ease, currency)
Identify gaps and barriers to use	■ Note any indications of 'hidden' or little known holdings ■ Document the conditions for use of each repository ■ Indicate suitability for wider use vs. requirements for mediation
2. Current Practices in Knowledge Sharing	
Assess formal tools	■ Obtain employee opinions (in interviews) regarding existing internal sharing tools ■ Identify current effectiveness, desired features/ functionality
Identify typical practices	■ Trace communication patterns across business teams ■ Identify at-risk knowledge (e.g. impending retirements, turnover)
Identify 'silos'	■ Identify instances where connections between teams are weaker than ideal

3. Findings and Recommendations	
Prepare report for stakeholder review	■ Prepare a findings report and derive draft recommendations ■ Share report with stakeholders for review ■ Discuss implications with stakeholders
Finalize, get approval, build implementation plan	■ Adjust recommendations according to review ■ Obtain executive committee approval ■ Prepare high level implementation schedule for recommendations ■ Estimate resource requirements

While corporate standards may have some impact on how we format our written materials, the simple examples shown here illustrate that we always have visual options for helping our audience understand what we are communicating.

▶▶▶ *WHAT DO YOU THINK, ANYA AND ERIC?*

Anya and Eric are applying to a graduate information program. Anya has a background in biology and has worked in a medical laboratory. Eric has a background in history and has worked in the admissions office of a private academy.

> **Eric:** Your examples strike me because of all the documentation I have handled in my job. I have seen some absolutely awful applications and letters, and I totally get why communicating information is a matter of elegance in content and in looks. Honing my skills here will surely stand me in good stead in my new career.
>
> **Anya:** Of course, in the lab most information is managed using forms—but I have in fact noticed that some of the forms we used were badly designed, wasting our time.
>
> *(Cont'd)*

Could you give some examples how documents or forms executed poorly had a negative impact?

Eric: I noticed many times how an applicant with fantastic qualifications more or less hid them—not intentionally of course—behind poor writing and a hard-to-read and clumsy appearance. In order to give the kid a chance, I felt obliged to create a summary for the admissions committee to highlight the main points to consider.

Anya: One of the forms we use all the time takes up just over one page. It could easily fit on one page with a bit of tweaking—but no, we have to lift page 1 to get to page 2, thirty times a day. It's a minor annoyance, but I'm thinking how much time it would save us in the aggregate—not to mention cut in half the volume of paper filed—if the form were redone by someone skilled in document layout.

Eric: Conversely, the academy's promotional collateral could use some love. It looks as if an amateur created it, and I don't think it speaks well of the quality of the academic program.

Anya: I'm thinking we could maintain the accuracy of our work in the lab but increase throughput in each process if the forms we use were given a makeover for clarity. I'm used to it now, but in the beginning the ambiguous or vague terminology on some forms confused me and I had to take extra time to double check I was doing things correctly.

What about communication of policy or process?

Anya: Oh dear. You can imagine how critical it is to understand every nuance of process and practice in a medical lab, and I certainly remember times when I had that "huh?" reaction and had to ask colleagues what was actually being said in a process description. The writing was just so inept, it wasn't funny. OK, I realize the descriptions came from scientists and we don't exactly need high literature here, but still. I once took a red pen to a particularly egregious example and showed to some colleagues how much clearer the text could be, but I was

(Cont'd)

told not to bother as that had been tried before and wasn't welcome on the part of the creator. I remember thinking, "Really? Someone takes offense at being shown an improvement that would help the entire lab?"

Eric: Tell me about it. The instructions for filling in the academy's application form are so convoluted and confusing it's a wonder we don't have to send them all back or walk the parents through it step by step over the phone. I think I'll risk it—seeing that, with any luck, I'll soon be back in school—and offer my supervisor a proposed revision. Perhaps if I frame it by saying "it would reflect well on the academy if our application instructions were really clear and easy to follow" I might avoid the kind of untoward reaction you mention, Anya.

Am I hearing that some time in the future when you two become managers, you will insist on high quality in the communications issued by your teams?

Eric: You bet. As you said, Anya, it's not as if we need superbly polished prose for every quick message, but there is no reason to tolerate the waste of time and annoyance resulting from bad writing.

Anya: My experience in the lab tells me that in any role I might hold in my career, it will be a good idea to take a close look at each and every item employees use to guide their work **and** each and every item customers see—be that signage, bills, product manuals, what have you. Come to think of it, that goes for announcements, too. It drives me crazy when I hear the conductor in the commuter train on the PA system saying "On behalf of myself and the rest of the crew, you are asked not to cross the tracks as that is prohibited and illegal"—wow, three problems in one brief statement!

Eric: I never articulated it for myself in these terms, but now that I think about it, quality in communication is part of an organization's brand, isn't it?

Anya: And part of a professional's brand!

Music to my ears ...

Postscript

It is my hope that dipping into the book has provided you with suggestions for further thinking and discussion with colleagues about your own career and about the collective prospects for our many kinds of information professions.

For now, I leave you with a few suggestions for simple habits anyone may build into his or her normal life. Keep them in the back of your mind—better yet, share them with others:

- Use—or create—opportunities to ask your peers about their careers and future professional plans. Of course, you will offer your own thoughts and, if possible, suggest resources they may not yet have found.

- Keep an open radar to monitor overall perception of members of our profession: From media coverage to dinner conversations, you will be able to pick up on subtle signals. Look for opportunities to offer journalists the material they need for creating "did you know" type pieces about information professional roles not familiar to a mainstream audience.

- Look for opportunities to tell the story about what you do in your professional capacity to members of other professions. Vignettes focusing on how you and your colleagues facilitate business results may intrigue listeners and potentially raise the thought in their minds "wonder if my team could use someone with Doris' skills"?

- As you progress in your career, share the stories from your job experience with students and younger colleagues to help expand their view of what falls within an information professional's career.

One day, perhaps you will join the ranks of writers who support and inspire fellow professionals and students. Perhaps you will organize and speak at events intended to galvanize members of the information profession to communicate broadly about our roles. Perhaps you will have your part in raising society's awareness of our value.

As I have said on the many occasions when someone expressed appreciation for something I had offered: I ask for nothing other than that you pass it on!

Additional Reading

Cutshaw, O. (2011). *Recovery, reframing, and renewal: Surviving an information science career crisis in a time of change.* Oxford, UK: Chandos Publishing.

de Stricker, U., & Hurst-Wahl, J. (2011). *The information and knowledge professional's career handbook: Define and create your success.* Oxford, UK: Chandos Publishing.

Dority, G. K. (2012). *LIS career sourcebook: Managing and maximizing every step of your career.* Santa Barbara, CA: Libraries Unlimited.

Greer, R. C., Grover, R. J., & Fowler, S. G. (2013). *Introduction to the library and information professions* (2nd). Santa Barbara, CA: Libraries Unlimited.

Hunt, D., & Grossman, D. (2013). *The librarian's skillbook: 51 essential career skills for information professionals.* San Leandro, CA: Information Edge.

Lankes, D. (2011). *The atlas of new librarianship.* Cambridge, MA: MIT Press.

Lawson, J., Kroll, J., & Kowatch, K. (2010). *The new information professional: Your guide to careers in the digital age.* New York, NY: Neal-Schuman Publishers.

Markgren, S., & Allen, T. E. (2013). *Career Q&A: A librarian's real-life practical guide to managing a successful career.* Medford, NJ: Information Today.

Mavrinac, M. A., & Stymest, K. (2012). *Pay it forward: Mentoring new information professionals.* Chicago, IL: Association of College and Research Libraries.

McCormack, N., & Cotter, C. (2013). *Managing burnout in the workplace: A guide for information professionals.* Oxford, UK: Chandos Publishing.

McKnight, M. (2010). *The Agile librarian's guide to thriving in any institution.* Santa Barbara, CA: Libraries Unlimited.

Ptolomey, J. (2008). *Taking charge of your career: A guide for the library and information professional.* Oxford, UK: Chandos Publishing.

Ruddock, B. (2012). *The new professional's toolkit.* London, UK: Facet Publications.

Shontz, P., & Murray, R. (2012). *What do employers want?* Santa Barbara, CA: Libraries Unlimited.

Index

Note: Page numbers followed by *b* indicate boxes.